Tia's Sweet Tooth Making Sweet Memories

Sharing My Journey and Passion for Baking and Cake Decorating

SHATIA GODFREY

Foreword by J.M. Conigliaro

DEDICATION

Dedicated to Dreamers, Baking Enthusiasts, families, and baking professionals.

May this cookbook be your guiding light in the sweet dance of baking delights. May your kitchen or bake shop be filled with warmth, joy, and the irresistible aroma of freshly baked dreams.

Dear Sweet Reader,

When it comes to baking, the quality of your ingredients can make all the difference between a *good* dessert and an *extraordinary* one. However, remember that baking is for everyone, so if you can't find the best ingredients, do not hesitate to try your best and bake away. Selecting the best ingredients you can find is important for several reasons:

- **Flavor:** High-quality ingredients, such as fresh butter, real vanilla extract, and premium chocolate, have richer, more deep and nuanced flavors. Premium ingredients infuse your baked goods with depth and complexity, making every bite a delight.
- **Texture:** Great ingredients contribute to the desired texture of your baked goods. Fresh eggs, for example, make fluffy cakes and soufflés that rise perfectly. Similarly, using high-quality flour ensures that the crumb in your pastries and bread is tender, smooth, and scrumptious.
- **Consistency:** Superior ingredients offer better consistency, meaning your recipes will turn out beautifully every time you try to make them. This means it is reliable, and it allows you to bake with confidence, knowing the outcome will meet high standards.
- **Nutrition:** Quality ingredients are often more nutritious and better for your health. It is very important to stay healthy. Organic and non-GMO products, for example, can provide better health benefits since they have fewer additives. This means you're not just creating something delicious but also something wholesome.

Investing in great ingredients is an investment in the success of your baking. It transforms your efforts into creations that not only taste fantastic but also bring joy to everyone who tries them. So next time you bake, choose the best ingredients you can find—your taste buds will thank you.

Happy Baking!

Warm regards,

Shatia Godfrey

Contents

PREFACE

Life is like a story, and you are the main character. In stories, characters face hardships, but they also manage to overcome them by learning from them. In life, you will have both joy and laughter but they also have tears and stress. It is in these negative moments that you can learn and grow the most.

You must know that you can face storms and come out of the bad parts of your life feeling renewed and still having hope. You have the power to change your circumstances and chase your dreams.

In my life, I have faced many challenges that brought me down. Through them, I found that what helped me the most was baking and decorating cakes. It was when I was using sugar and flour when I was kneading dough and when I was mixing icing that I felt the most at peace. It made me feel calm and energized. This is how I discovered that baking was both a passion and a safe space for me. This was how I could use my creativity while also making others and myself happy.

When I started out, I was not very good at baking, but I kept at it and practiced hard. Eventually, baking became second nature to me, and I was able to whip up a recipe in minutes and have perfectly baked goods each time I tried. I transformed my passion into a flourishing business and, in doing so, proved that I could overcome adversity.

Now, with these achievements under my belt, I am filled with gratitude—gratitude for the challenges that tested me, the setbacks that strengthened me, and the dreams that fueled my journey forward.

So, to all who dare to dream amidst the chaos of life, who refuse to be defined by their circumstances, and who embrace the power of resilience—this book is for you. May it serve as a lesson that within every struggle lies the potential for growth, and within every setback lies the opportunity for resilience to flourish.

Hold fast to your dreams. They are the guiding stars that illuminate the path forward. Above all, trust in your ability to overcome, for within you lies the strength to write your own story of triumph.

There is no limit to what you can achieve.

So, dear reader, embark on your journey with courage and conviction, knowing that the best is yet to come.

ACKNOWLEDGMENTS

As I poured my heart into crafting this cookbook, my thoughts couldn't help but drift to the remarkable human beings who have inspired me on my journey toward loving baking and the cultivation of the desire to share that passion through this book.

To all those who have been part of this journey, I want to express my deepest gratitude. Your belief in me, your support, and your love have guided me through even the darkest times of my life.

To my grandmother, Veronica who holds a special place in my heart, I extend my gratitude. She not only taught me the art of baking but also instilled in me the values of hard work, determination, and resilience. Her kitchen was the site of the beginning of my passion and became my sanctuary.

To my high school baking teacher, Judith Conigliaro, your passion for cake decorating and baking ignited a spark within me that continues to burn brightly to this day. Your belief in my potential gave me the courage to pursue my dreams. Thank you.

To Pam, my dear friend, your entrepreneurial spirit and creativity showed me that baking and cake decorating could be more than just a hobby. You are the one who inspired me to start my business. Your infectious enthusiasm and unwavering support sustained me through the toughest of times. I will forever cherish the memories we shared.

To Pastor Ingrid, your faith in me has kept me steadfast and thankful throughout my life with each decision and milestone. Your gentle encouragement reminded me that sometimes the things we love most are worth fighting for.

And to my beloved husband, your love, support, and encouragement are invaluable. Your belief in me has been a constant source of strength and inspiration. I am endlessly grateful to have you by my side as our lives transform together.

To everyone who has touched my life in some way, whether through a kind word, a shared moment, or a simple gesture of support, I offer my deepest thanks. You have made this journey richer, sweeter, and more meaningful than I ever could have imagined.

FOREWORD

Shatia Brown was one of hundreds of students I was blessed to introduce to the art of Commercial Baking during my 32 years of teaching in the Baltimore City Public School System. Her book, "Tia's Sweet Tooth - Making Sweet Memories Sharing My Journey and Passion for Baking and Cake Decorating," is a collection of recipes, inspirational stories, and memories of her baking and cake decorating journey.

She was one of my beginner Commercial Baking students in September 2002. Shatia (as I knew her until she graduated in June 2005) quickly mastered the sanitation, safety, and equipment operation competencies, as well as how to measure and scale ingredients in commercial quantities. She eagerly learned to make cakes, pies, cookies, breads, icings, toppings, and our most popular product.... doughnuts. But her passion was always cake decorating. She appeared to have a natural talent and would frequently help other classmates who were struggling with a particular decorating skill (which I appreciated greatly).

Shatia developed an interest in baking at the tender age of thirteen. She watched her grandmother bake cakes, cookies, and pies and helped sell the treats outside her grandmother's apartment building. She told me that her grandmother was always her inspiration.

After graduating from the Commercial Baking program at Mergenthaler Vocational Technical High School, she immediately entered the Applied Science Professional Baking and Pastry program at the Baltimore International College, where she earned her associate degree.

Shatia Godfrey is now the owner/operator of Tia's Sweet Tooth LLC and has plans to open a custom cake shop with the same name. Her strides in following her dream should inspire others who have similar hopes or interests. This book will be an asset to those considering advancing their baking skills and an enjoyable and fun read for those interested in baking as a hobby.

J. M. Conigliaro

Commercial Baking Instructor

1977-2009

CHAPTER 1: CAKES

Grandma Made Me a Candy-Cake

When I think back on what started my passion for baking, one particular memory comes to mind. I was 8 years old, wide-eyed and full of enthusiasm. My grandmother lovingly baked a cake for me, but I knew that it was not just a cake; it was her way of gifting me all of her affection and love. Her affection for me was infused into every crumb and frosted swirl on the cake.

I remember that it was a humble yellow cake, but I knew that its warmth was one that would only come if made by my grandmother over and with her hands. It was only when I started eating it that I learnt what a masterpiece the cake truly was. It was a treasure trove of candies nestled within its tender layers and on the outside of the cake, a surprise waiting to be discovered with each slice.

My grandmother, who knew all about my ginormous sweet tooth, had poured her whole heart and the extent of her creativity into that cake. Each layer had something different - Skittles, Laffy Taffy, and all the beloved candies that I loved so much as a child growing up in the 90s.

But, of course, the secret ingredient was love.

As I ate the cake, my heart overflowed with gratitude for my grandmother. This is a memory I hold dear. It is because of her that I now love baking and have made it a huge part of my life.

Every time I make a cake, I think of you. Thank you, Grandma.

Grandma's Candy Cake

Ingredients

- ½ cup of butter (1 stick), unsalted (room temperature)
- 3 cups all-purpose flour (sifted)
- 1 ½ cups sugar (granulated)
- ½ tsp salt
- ½ cup of canola or vegetable oil
- 4 large eggs (room temperature)
- 1 Tbsp baking powder
- 1 Tbsp vanilla extract
- 1 cup Jimmy rainbow sprinkles
- A lot of your favorite candies!

Paired well with Vanilla Buttercream – Recipe in Chapter 2

Directions

1. Make sure all ingredients are measured.

2. Turn oven to 325 degrees F.

3. Grease an 8-inch cake pan with cake pan spray (with flour) generously or line a cupcake pan with liners.

4. In a separate bowl, whisk flour, baking powder, and salt.

5. Cream together butter, oil, and sugar until creamy and pale in color.

6. Add eggs, one by one, until completely mixed. Be sure to scrape the sides of the bowl.

7. Stir in vanilla extract.

8. Alternate by starting and ending with the flour and adding buttermilk to the egg mixture. Combine until incorporated. Don't over-mix!

9. Add in the 1 cup of rainbow Jimmy sprinkles and mix the sprinkles with a spoon until mixed.

10. Evenly divide the batter evenly between both cake pans and bake for 30-40 minutes. Be sure to complete the cake test.

11. When done, cool for 10 minutes on a wire rack. Enjoy!

Cake test: Use a skewer, toothpick, or knife and gently stick it in the center of the cake. If the tool you use comes out clean, then the cake is done. If not, bake until the tool you use comes out clean.

* *See the Icing/ Glaze/Fondant chapter if you want to top the cake with a glaze or simple syrup.*

Chocolate Dream Cake

Ingredients

- 1 3/4 cups all-purpose flour (sifted)
- 3/4 cup unsweetened cocoa powder
- 1 1/2 tsp baking powder
- 1 1/2 tsp baking soda
- 1 tsp salt
- 2 cups granulated sugar
- 2 large eggs at room temperature
- 1 cup whole milk
- 1/2 cup vegetable oil
- 2 teaspoons vanilla extract
- 1 cup strong brewed espresso or coffee, cooled

Paired well with any Icing recipe in Chapter 2

Directions

1. Make sure all ingredients are measured.
2. Turn oven to 350°F (175°C).
3. Grease and flour two 9-inch round cake pans, or line them with parchment paper or line a cupcake pan with liners.
4. In a large mixing bowl, sift together the flour, cocoa powder, baking powder, baking soda, salt, and granulated sugar.
5. In another bowl, whisk together the eggs, milk, vegetable oil, and vanilla extract until well combined.
6. Gradually add the wet ingredients to the dry ingredients, mixing until smooth and well combined.
7. Stir in the cooled brewed espresso or coffee until the batter is smooth.
8. Divide the batter evenly between the prepared cake pans.
9. Bake in the preheated oven for 25-30 minutes or until a toothpick inserted into the center of the cakes comes out clean.
10. Remove the cakes from the oven and allow them to cool in the pans for 15 minutes before transferring them to a wire rack to cool completely.

Cake test: Use a skewer, toothpick, or knife and gently stick it in the center of the cake. If the tool you use comes out clean, then the cake is done. If not, bake until the tool you use comes out clean.

* *See the Icing/ Glaze/Fondant chapter if you want to top the cake with a glaze or simple syrup.*

Vanilla Cloud Delight

Ingredients

- 3 cups all-purpose flour (sifted)
- 1 ½ cups sugar (granulated)
- ½ cup (1 stick) of butter, unsalted (room temperature)
- ½ tsp salt
- ½ cup of canola or vegetable oil
- 4 large eggs (room temperature)
- 1 Tbsp baking powder
- 1 ¼ cup of buttermilk (room temperature)
- 1 Tbsp vanilla extract or vanilla bean paste

Paired well with any Icing recipe in Chapter 2

Directions

1. Make sure all ingredients are measured.

2. Turn oven to 325 degrees F.

3. Grease 8-inch cake pans with cake pan spray (with flour) generously or line the cupcake pan with liners.

4. In a separate bowl, whisk flour, baking powder, and salt.

5. Cream together butter, oil, and sugar until creamy and pale in color.

6. Add eggs, one by one, until completely mixed. Be sure to scrape the sides of the bowl.

7. Stir in vanilla extract.

8. Alternate by starting and ending with the flour and adding buttermilk to the egg mixture. Combine until incorporated. Don't over-mix!

9. Evenly divide the batter evenly between both cake pans and bake for 30-40 minutes. Be sure to complete the cake test.

10. When done, cool for 10 minutes on a wire rack. Enjoy!

Cake test: Use a skewer, toothpick, or knife and gently stick it in the center of the cake. If the tool you use comes out clean, then the cake is done. If not, bake until the tool you use comes out clean.

* *See the Icing/ Glaze/Fondant Chapter 2 if you want to top the cake with a glaze or simple syrup.*

Lemon Sunshine Bliss

Ingredients

- 1 1/2 cups all-purpose flour (sifted)
- 1 tsp baking powder
- 1/2 tsp baking soda
- 1/4 tsp salt
- 3/4 cup granulated sugar
- 2 large eggs at room temperature
- 1/2 cup vegetable oil
- 1/2 cup sour cream
- 1/4 cup freshly squeezed lemon juice
- 2 Tbsp lemon zest
- 1 tsp vanilla extract

Directions

1. Make sure all ingredients are measured.
2. Turn oven to 350°F (175°C).
3. Grease and flour a 9-inch round cake pan or line the cupcake pan with liners.
4. In a medium bowl, whisk together the flour, baking powder, baking soda, and salt. Set aside.
5. In a large bowl, beat together the granulated sugar and eggs until pale and fluffy, about 2 minutes.
6. Slowly add the vegetable oil while continuing to beat the mixture until well combined and smooth.
7. Mix in the sour cream, lemon juice, lemon zest, and vanilla extract until incorporated.
8. Gradually add the dry ingredients to the wet ingredients, mixing until just combined. Be careful not to overmix.
9. Pour the batter into the prepared cake pan and spread it evenly with a spatula.
10. Bake in the preheated oven for 25-30 minutes or until a toothpick inserted into the center comes out clean.
11. Allow the cake to cool in the pan for 10 minutes, then transfer it to a wire rack to cool completely.

Cake test: Use a skewer, toothpick, or knife and gently stick it in the center of the cake. If the tool you use comes out clean, then the cake is done. If not, bake until the tool you use comes out clean.

See the Icing/ Glaze/Fondant Chapter 2 if you want to top the cake with a glaze or simple syrup.

Golden Pound Cake

Ingredients

- 3 cups all-purpose flour (sifted)
- 1 cup (2 sticks) of butter, unsalted (room temperature)
- 3 cups sugar
- 6 eggs (room temperature)
- 1 Tbsp vanilla extract
- 2 cups heavy whipping cream

Directions

1. Make sure all ingredients are measured.
2. Turn oven to 325 degrees F.
3. Grease Bundt pan or 9-inch cake pans with cake pan spray (with flour) generously or line the cupcake pan with liners.
4. Cream butter and sugar on medium speed until its fluffy and light in color (pale color). Be sure to scrape the sides of the bowl.
5. Add eggs, one by one, until completely mixed.

6. Add flour one cup at a time and alternate using the heavy whipping cream at a time until all is completely mixed (be sure to start with the flour and end with the flour).

7. Add vanilla extract on low speed until it is combined. Don't over-mix!

8. Pour batter into Bundt pan and bake for 1-1/2 hours or until the cake test comes out clean.

9. When done, cool for 10 minutes on a wire rack. Enjoy!

Cake test: Use a skewer, toothpick, or knife and gently stick it in the center of the cake. If the tool you use comes out clean, then the cake is done. If not, bake until the tool you use comes out clean.

* *See the Icing/ Glaze/Fondant Chapter 2 if you want to top the cake with a glaze or simple syrup.*

Velvety Cream Pound Cake

Ingredients

- 3 cups all-purpose flour (sifted)
- 1 cup (2 sticks) of butter, unsalted (room temperature)
- 3 cups sugar (granulated)
- 6 eggs
- ¼ cup vegetable oil
- 1 cup sour cream
- ½ tsp baking powder
- 2 tsp vanilla extract (or you may use lemon or almond extract)

Directions

1. Make sure all ingredients are measured.
2. Turn oven to 325 degrees F.
3. Grease Bundt pan or 9-inch cake pans with cake pan spray (with flour) generously.

4. Cream butter and sugar on medium speed until its fluffy and light in color (pale color). Be sure to scrape the sides of the bowl.

5. Add eggs, one by one, until completely mixed. Be sure to scrape down the sides and bottom of the bowl.

6. Add sour cream alternating with the flour (be sure to start with the flour and end with the flour). Mix until all is incorporated.

7. Add vanilla extract on low speed until combined. Don't over-mix!

8. Pour batter into Bundt pan and bake for 1-1/2 hours or until the cake test comes out clean.

9. When done, cool for 10 minutes on a wire rack. Enjoy!

Cake test: Use a skewer, toothpick, or knife and gently stick it in the center of the cake. If the tool you use comes out clean, then the cake is done. If not, bake until the tool you use comes out clean.

* See the Icing/ Glaze/Fondant Chapter 2 if you want to top the cake with a glaze or simple syrup.

"Making Cakes Motivation Time"

"Baking a cake isn't just about following a recipe—it's about expressing yourself, being patient, and putting in a bit of heart. From gathering your ingredients to adding that last touch of frosting, every step is a chance to make something uniquely yours, to make something special. Just like life, things may not always go as planned—maybe the cake doesn't rise quite right, or the frosting turns out a little uneven, but that's where you get to shine, where you get to learn, adapt, and improve!

As long as you have the passion and determination, every time you dive into the fun of cake-making, remember: you've got what it takes. You have the creativity to try new flavors, the patience to improve your skills, and the confidence to take on any challenge. Embrace every step, enjoy it, and you will get results (and some tasty treats).

When you share your creations with others, infuse it with love and joy, so you can enjoy even the simplest moments in life while allowing others to enjoy it too.

Keep baking, keep believing, and let each cake inspire others to appreciate the little things! You got this! "

– Shatia Godfrey

Veronica's Lemon Pound Cake

Ingredients

- 3 cups all-purpose flour (sifted)
- 1 cup (2 sticks) of butter unsalted, softened
- 2 cups granulated sugar
- 4 large eggs at room temperature
- 1/2 Tbsp lemon zest (from about 1 lemon)
- 1 tsp vanilla extract
- ½ tsp lemon extract
- 1/2 tsp baking powder
- 1/2 tsp baking soda
- 1/2 tsp salt
- 1 cup sour cream
- 1/4 cup of canola or vegetable oil

Paired well with Whipped Cream Cheese Icing Chapter 2.

Directions

1. Make sure all ingredients are measured.

2. Turn oven to 350°F (175°C).

3. Grease and flour a Bundt pan.

4. In a large bowl, whisk together the sugar, eggs, lemon zest, vegetable oil, and vanilla extract until well combined.

5. In a separate bowl, sift together the flour, baking powder, baking soda, and salt.

6. Gradually add the dry ingredients to the wet ingredients, alternating with the sour cream and lemon juice. Begin and end with the dry ingredients, mixing until just combined.

7. Pour the batter into the prepared Bundt pan and smooth the top with a spatula.

8. Bake in the preheated oven for 50-60 minutes or until a toothpick inserted into the center comes out clean.

9. Allow the cake to cool in the pan for 15 minutes, then transfer to a wire rack to cool completely.

Cake test: Use a skewer, toothpick, or knife and gently stick it in the center of the cake. If the tool you use comes out clean, then the cake is done. If not, bake until the tool you use comes out clean.

* See the Icing/ Glaze/Fondant Chapter 2 if you want to top the cake with a glaze or simple syrup.*

Veronica's Carrot Cake

Ingredients

- 2 cups all-purpose flour (sifted)
- 1 1/2 cups granulated sugar
- 1 tsp baking powder
- 1/2 tsp baking soda
- 1/2 tsp salt
- 1 tsp ground cinnamon
- 1/2 tsp ground nutmeg
- 1/2 tsp ground ginger
- 1/4 tsp ground cloves
- 3 large eggs at room temperature
- 3/4 cup vegetable oil
- 1 tsp vanilla extract
- 2 cups grated carrots (about 3 medium carrots)
- 1/2 cup crushed pineapple, drained

- 1/2 cup chopped walnuts or pecans (optional)
- 1/2 cup raisins (optional)

Paired well with Cream Cheese Icing Chapter 2.

Directions

1. Make sure all ingredients are measured.
2. Turn oven to 350°F (175°C).
3. Grease and flour a 9x13 inch baking pan, or line it with parchment paper or line cupcake pans with liners.
4. In a large mixing bowl, whisk together the flour, sugar, baking powder, baking soda, salt, cinnamon, nutmeg, ginger, and cloves until well combined.
5. In another bowl, beat the eggs, then add in the vegetable oil and vanilla extract. Mix until smooth.
6. Gradually add the wet ingredients to the dry ingredients, stirring until just combined.
7. Fold in the grated carrots, crushed pineapple, nuts (if using), and raisins (if using) until evenly distributed throughout the batter.
8. Pour the batter into the prepared baking pan and spread it out evenly.
9. Bake in the preheated oven for 35-40 minutes or until a toothpick inserted into the center comes out clean.
10. Allow the cake to cool completely in the pan on a wire rack.
11. While the cake is cooling, prepare the whipped cream cheese frosting that's in the icing chapter.

Cake test: Use a skewer, toothpick, or knife and gently stick it in the center of the cake. If the tool you use comes out clean, then the cake is done. If not, bake until the tool you use comes out clean.

* See the Icing/ Glaze/Fondant Chapter 2 if you want to top the cake with a glaze or simple syrup.*

Tropical Turnover Delight

Ingredients

- 1 1/2 cups all-purpose flour (sifted)
- 1/2 cup (1 stick) of butter unsalted (room temperature)
- 1 cup packed light brown sugar
- 1 can (20 ounces) pineapple slices in juice, drained (reserve juice)
- Maraschino cherries, drained
- 1 1/2 tsp baking powder
- 1/2 tsp salt
- 1/2 cup granulated sugar
- 2 large eggs
- 1 tsp vanilla extract
- 1/2 cup pineapple juice (reserved from the canned pineapple
- 1/4 cup milk

Directions

1. Make sure all ingredients are measured.

2. Turn oven to 350°F (175°C).

3. Melt the butter in a 9-inch round cake pan in the oven.

4. Sprinkle the brown sugar evenly over the melted butter in the pan.

5. Arrange pineapple slices on top of the brown sugar. Place a cherry in the center of each pineapple slice and any gaps between slices.

6. In a medium bowl, whisk together flour, baking powder, and salt.

7. In another bowl, beat granulated sugar and eggs until light and fluffy. Stir in vanilla extract.

8. Gradually add the flour mixture to the egg mixture, alternating with pineapple juice and milk, beginning and ending with the flour mixture. Mix until just combined.

9. Pour the batter evenly over the pineapple slices and smooth the top.

10. Bake for 45-50 minutes or until a toothpick inserted into the center comes out clean.

11. Allow the cake to cool in the pan for 15 minutes, then carefully invert it onto a serving plate.

Cake test: Use a skewer, toothpick, or knife and gently stick it in the center of the cake. If the tool you use comes out clean, then the cake is done. If not, bake until the tool you use comes out clean.

* *See the Icing/ Glaze/Fondant chapter if you want to top the cake with a glaze or simple syrup.*

Zesty Citrus Cascade Cake

Ingredients

- 3 cups cake flour (sifted)
- 1 ½ cups (3 sticks) butter, unsalted (room temperature)
- 3 cups granulated sugar
- 1 tsp salt
- 5 large eggs (room temperature)
- 1 cup 7UP soda (room temperature)
- 1 Tbsp lemon extract
- 2 tsp Lemon zest

Directions

1. Make sure all ingredients are measured.
2. Turn oven to 325 degrees F.
3. Grease Bundt pan or 9-inch cake pans with cake pan spray (with flour) generously.
4. Cream butter on medium speed for 2 minutes.

5. Gradually add sugar and salt. Cream all three ingredients for about an additional 5 minutes or until the creamed ingredients are pale in color and fluffy.

6. Add eggs, one by one, until completely mixed. Be sure to scrape down the sides and bottom of the bowl.

7. Turn the mixer on low speed and slowly add flour.

8. Add the 7UP, lemon extract, and lemon zest.

9. Scrape the sides of the bowl and mix with a spatula until incorporated. Don't over-mix!

10. Pour batter into cake pan and bake for 1-1/2 hours or until the cake test comes out clean.

11. When done, cool for 10 minutes on a wire rack. Enjoy!

Cake test: Use a skewer, toothpick, or knife and gently stick it in the center of the cake. If the tool you use comes out clean, then the cake is done. If not, bake until the tool you use comes out clean.

* See the Icing/ Glaze/Fondant Chapter 2 if you want to top the cake with a glaze or simple syrup.

Midnight Cookies & Cream Delight

Ingredients

- 2 cups all-purpose flour (sifted)
- 1 cup granulated sugar
- 1 cup milk
- 1/2 cup vegetable oil
- 2 large eggs
- 2 tsp baking powder
- 1 tsp vanilla extract
- 12 Oreo cookies crushed into small pieces

Paired well with Cookies & Cream Buttercream Chapter 2.

Directions

1. Make sure all ingredients are measured.
2. Turn oven to 350°F (175°C).
3. Grease and flour two 9-inch round cake pans, or line a cupcake pan with liners.

4. In a large mixing bowl, combine flour, sugar, baking powder, and crushed Oreo cookies.

5. In another bowl, whisk together milk, vegetable oil, eggs, and vanilla extract until well combined.

6. Gradually add the wet ingredients to the dry ingredients, mixing until just combined.

7. Divide the batter evenly between the prepared cake pans.

8. Bake in the preheated oven for 25-30 minutes or until a toothpick inserted into the center comes out clean.

9. Allow the cakes to cool in the pans for 10 minutes, then transfer them to a wire rack to cool completely.

10. While the cakes are cooling, prepare the frosting. In a chilled mixing bowl, beat the heavy cream, powdered sugar, and vanilla extract until stiff peaks form. Gently fold in the crushed Oreo cookies.

11. Once the cakes are completely cooled, place one cake layer on a serving plate or cake stand. Spread a layer of frosting evenly over the top.

Cake test: Use a skewer, toothpick, or knife and gently stick it in the center of the cake. If the tool you use comes out clean, then the cake is done. If not, bake until the tool you use comes out clean.

* *See the Icing/ Glaze/Fondant chapter if you want to top the cake with a glaze or simple syrup.*

Scarlet Velvety Cake

Ingredients

- 14 oz all-purpose flour (sifted)
- 6 oz butter, unsalted (melted but not hot)
- 14 oz sugar (granulated)
- 2 Tbsp cocoa powder
- 1 tsp salt
- 1 tsp baking soda
- 2 eggs (room temp)
- 4 oz vegetable oil
- 8 oz buttermilk (room temp)
- 1 Tbsp white vinegar
- 1 tsp vanilla
- 1 Tbsp Red Velvet extract
- 1 Tbsp super red food coloring

Paired well with Whipped Cream Cheese Icing or Cream Cheese Icing, Chapter 2

Directions

1. Make sure all ingredients are measured.

2. Turn oven on 325 degrees F.

3. Grease 8-inch cake pans with cake pan spray (with flour) generously or line the cupcake pan with liners.

4. In a separate bowl, whisk together eggs, oil, buttermilk, vinegar, melted butter, and food coloring.

5. Add flour, sugar, baking soda, cocoa powder, and salt into the mixing bowl with the paddle attachment and mix until incorporated.

6. Add the wet mixture that's in the separate bowl to the dry mixture and mix until all is combined. Be sure to scrape down the sides and bottom of the bowl. Mix until combined.

7. Divide the batter evenly between both cake pans and bake for 30-40 minutes. Be sure to complete the cake test.

8. When done, cool for 10 minutes on a wire rack. Enjoy!

Cake test: Use a skewer, toothpick, or knife and gently stick it in the center of the cake. If the tool you use comes out clean, then the cake is done. If not, bake until the tool you use comes out clean.

* See the Icing/ Glaze/Fondant, Chapter 2 if you want to top the cake with a glaze or simple syrup

CHAPTER 2:
ICINGS/GLAZES/FONDANT

The bell chimed, signaling the start of another day at Mergenthaler Vocational-Technical Senior High School. Immediately and hurriedly, I made my way to the bakeshop. I stood at my station dressed in my uniform: crisp white uniform scrubs, white apron, and baker's hat with a hair net secured underneath. It was the middle of sophomore year; this year, we would finally study a method I had been eager to learn – creating icing from scratch.

I was nervous and excited. I gathered the ingredients listed on the recipe card: powdered sugar, shortening, vanilla extract, and butter-flavored extract. I measured each ingredient to the ounce as my head raced, filled with self-deprecating thoughts: you will never get this right; you are not good enough to bake.

The bakeshop hummed with activity, filled with all my classmates who busied themselves with their own baking projects. Despite the commotion; my focus remained solely on the task at hand. With a deep breath, I began creaming the block of shortening. Slowly but surely, I felt it morph until it formed a creamy texture.

I gradually added the powdered sugar, watching as the mixture transformed into a fluffy, pale concoction. The aroma of vanilla extract filled the air. I had done it! It smelled divine!

I held my breath, praying that I had achieved the perfect consistency. Slowly, the icing began to come together, smooth and creamy, just as the recipe described.

Finally, I tasted it. It was perfect – sweet, buttery, and utterly delicious!

At that moment, I knew that I had found my passion. Now, I share these learnings with you.

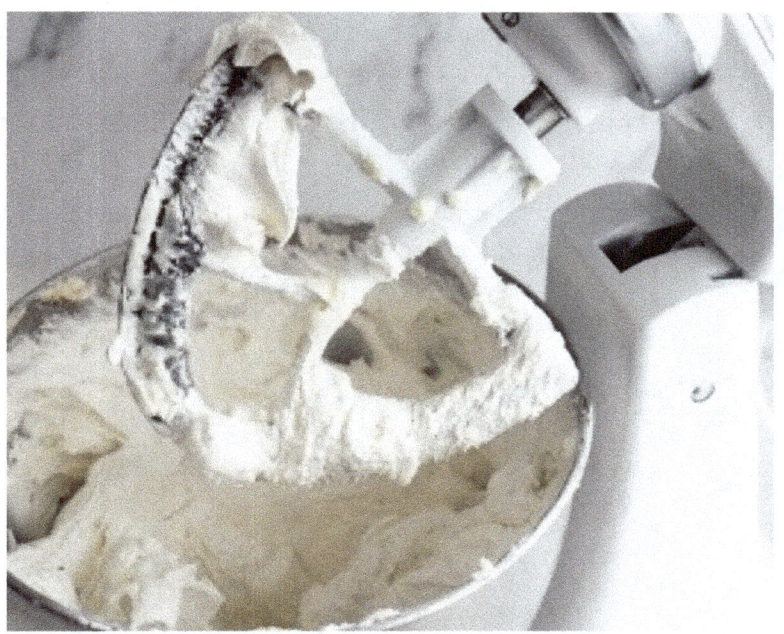

Vanilla Buttercream Icing

Ingredients

- 1 cup (2 sticks) of butter unsalted, softened
- 3 cups powdered sugar (sifted)
- 1 tsp vanilla extract or vanilla bean paste
- 3 Tbsp heavy whipping cream (I like it extra creamy)
- salt, pinch

Directions

1. Make sure all ingredients are measured.

2. In a stand mixer, cream the butter with a paddle attachment on medium speed for 5 minutes. Intermediately scrape the sides of the bowl and continue mixing. You will notice that the yellow butter will turn a pale color.

3. Be sure to turn off the mixer and add a cup at a time of powdered sugar. Mix on low speed until the butter and powdered sugar are blended, and scrape the sides of the bowl after incorporating each cup of powdered sugar.

4. Once all the powder sugar is added to the mixer, turn the mixer on medium speed and mix for 3-4 minutes.

5. Add in the heavy whipping cream, vanilla extract, and salt. Mix until light and fluffy.

6. If you want the icing to be creamier, add another Tbsp of heavy whipping cream.

Chocolate Buttercream Icing

Ingredients

- 1 cup (2 sticks) unsalted butter, softened
- 3 cups powdered sugar
- 1/2 cup unsweetened cocoa powder
- 1 tsp vanilla extract
- 1/4 cup heavy cream or milk

  Pinch of salt

Directions

1. Make sure all ingredients are measured.
2. In a large mixing bowl, beat the softened butter until creamy and smooth using a hand mixer or stand mixer fitted with a paddle attachment.
3. Gradually add in the powdered sugar, about 1 cup at a time, mixing well after each addition until smooth and fluffy.
4. Sift in the cocoa powder to remove any lumps and mix until fully incorporated with the butter and sugar mixture.

5. Add the vanilla extract and a pinch of salt and mix until combined.

6. Slowly pour in the heavy cream or milk while mixing on low speed, until the desired consistency is reached. You may need to adjust the amount of cream/milk depending on how thick or thin you prefer your buttercream.

7. Once everything is well combined and the buttercream is smooth and creamy, it's ready to use. If it's too thick, you can add a bit more cream/milk; if it's too thin, add more powdered sugar.

   Use the chocolate buttercream to frost cakes, cupcakes, or cookies, or simply enjoy it with a spoon!

Whipped Cream Cheese Icing

Ingredients

- 1 cup (2 sticks) of butter unsalted, softened
- 1 cup powdered sugar
- 1 tsp vanilla extract
- 2 cups heavy whipping cream cold

Directions

1. Make sure all ingredients are measured.
2. Beat cream cheese, powdered sugar, and vanilla until smooth and thick using a stand mixer- use the whisk attachment on a stand mixer.
3. While mixing your cream cheese mixture on medium-high speed, slowly add the heavy whipping cream. Adding slowly will avoid lumps.
4. Continue whipping until the frosting peaks are stiff. You will notice that the whipped cream looks a little thicker – that's how it should be.

Optional: You can add additional flavorings such as lemon zest, cocoa powder, or fruit extracts to customize the icing to your liking. Enjoy!

Cookies & Cream Buttercream

Ingredients

- 1 cup (2 sticks) of butter unsalted, softened
- 3 cups powdered sugar (sifted)
- 1 tsp vanilla extract or vanilla bean paste
- 3 Tbsp heavy whipping cream (I like it extra creamy)
- salt, pinch 12 Oreo cookies

Directions

1. Make sure all ingredients are measured.
2. Separate the icing from the Oreo cookie. You will add it to your butter.
3. Crush the Oreo into small pieces.
4. In a stand mixer, cream the butter with a paddle attachment on medium speed for 5 minutes. Intermediately scraping the sides of the bowl and continue mixing. You will notice that the yellow butter will turn a pale color.
5. Be sure to turn off the off the mixer and add a cup at a time of powdered sugar. Mix on low speed until the butter and

powdered sugar are blended, and scrape the sides of the bowl after incorporating each cup of powdered sugar.

6. Once all the powder sugar is added to the mixer, turn the mixer on medium speed and mix for 3-4 minutes.

7. Add in the heavy whipping cream, vanilla extract, and salt. Mix until light and fluffy.

8. Then add the crumbled Oreo cookies and mix until well incorporated.

9. If you want the icing to be creamier, add another Tbsp of heavy whipping cream.

Cream Cheese Icing

Ingredients

- 1 cup (2 sticks) of butter unsalted, softened
- 1/2 cup unsalted butter, softened
- 2 cups powdered sugar
- 1 tsp vanilla extract

Directions

1. Make sure all ingredients are measured.
2. In a mixing bowl, beat the softened cream cheese and butter together until smooth and creamy.
3. Gradually add the powdered sugar, mixing well after each addition until fully incorporated, and the icing is smooth.
4. Stir in the vanilla extract until evenly distributed throughout the icing.
5. If the icing is too thick, you can add a tablespoon of milk or cream at a time until you reach your desired consistency.
6. Once ready, use the icing to frost cakes, cupcakes, or any other baked goods of your choice.

"Making Icing Motivation Time"

"Creating icings, glazes, and fondant is more than just baking; it's a heartfelt expression of your love and creativity. As you blend ingredients, you're infusing each mixture with a piece of yourself.

In cake decorating, these components turn simple treats into stunning works of art. Every stroke of the spatula and delicate piping showcases your unique style and passion.

There will be challenges along the way—frustrating moments when things don't go as planned. But these setbacks provide valuable lessons that help you grow and improve.

Remember, your creations bring joy to others, whether it's a birthday cake with shimmering glaze or elegant wedding pastries. Embrace your kitchen as a realm of creativity, where humble ingredients become delightful treats. With each dessert, you're spreading moments of happiness and sweetness far and wide. You got this!"

– Shatia Godfrey

Lemon Buttercream

Ingredients

- 1 cup (2 sticks) unsalted butter, softened
- 4 cups powdered sugar
- 1 tsp lemon extract
- 1 teaspoon vanilla extract
- Pinch of salt
- 1-2 drops of yellow food color

Directions

1. Make sure all ingredients are measured.
2. In a large mixing bowl, beat the softened butter until creamy and smooth.
3. Gradually add the powdered sugar, one cup at a time, mixing well after each addition until smooth and creamy.
4. Add the lemon extract, vanilla extract, and a pinch of salt. Mix until well combined and smooth.

5. Taste and adjust the lemon flavor or sweetness, if desired, by adding more lemon juice or powdered sugar accordingly.

6. Once the desired consistency and flavor are achieved, the lemon buttercream icing is ready to use.

Spread or pipe the icing onto cooled cupcakes, cakes, or cookies.

Marshmallow Fondant

Ingredients

- 6 oz mini marshmallows
- 2-3 Tbsp water
- 2 lbs. powdered sugar (plus extra for dusting)
- 1/2 cup vegetable shortening for greasing and kneading
- Food coloring (optional)

Directions

1. Make sure all ingredients are measured.

2. In a microwave-safe bowl, combine the mini marshmallows and 2 tablespoons of water. Microwave in 30-second intervals, stirring in between, until the marshmallows are completely melted and smooth. If needed, add an additional tablespoon of water to achieve a smooth consistency.

3. Once the marshmallows are melted, gradually add in the powdered sugar, about 1 cup at a time, stirring with a greased spatula or wooden spoon until the mixture becomes too stiff to stir.

4. Grease your hands and a clean work surface generously with vegetable shortening to prevent sticking. Turn the marshmallow mixture out onto the greased surface.

5. Knead the mixture like dough, gradually incorporating the remaining powdered sugar until you achieve a smooth, elastic fondant. You may not need to use all the powdered sugar, depending on the consistency you desire.

6. If you want to add color to your fondant, knead in a few drops of food coloring until evenly distributed. Remember that the color will intensify over time, so add color gradually until you reach your desired shade.

7. Once the fondant is smooth and pliable, shape it into a ball and wrap it tightly in plastic wrap. Let it rest at room temperature for at least 1 hour to allow the fondant to firm up slightly.

8. After resting, your marshmallow fondant is ready to use! Roll it out on a surface dusted with powdered sugar to prevent sticking, then use it to cover cakes, create decorations, or sculpt figurines.

Any leftover fondant can be wrapped tightly in plastic wrap and stored in an airtight container at room temperature for up to 2 weeks. Before using leftover fondant, knead it again until smooth and pliable.

Vanilla Glaze

Ingredients

- 1 cup powdered sugar
- 2-3 Tbsp milk or cream
- 1 tsp vanilla extract

Directions

1. Make sure all ingredients are measured.
2. In a mixing bowl, sift the powdered sugar to remove any lumps.
3. Gradually add in the milk or cream, stirring continuously until you reach your desired consistency. You can adjust the amount of milk or cream depending on how thick or thin you want the glaze to be.
4. Stir in the vanilla extract until well combined.
5. If the glaze is too thick, add more milk or cream, a little at a time. If it's too thin, add more powdered sugar.
6. Once your glaze reaches the desired consistency, drizzle it over your baked goods, such as cakes, cookies, or donuts. Allow the glaze to set for a few minutes before serving.

Lemon Glaze

Ingredients

- 1 cup powdered sugar
- 2 Tbsp fresh lemon juice
- 1 tsp lemon zest

Directions

1. Make sure all ingredients are measured.
2. In a small bowl, whisk together the powdered sugar, lemon juice, and lemon zest until smooth and well combined.
3. If the glaze is too thick, add a little more lemon juice, 1 teaspoon at a time, until you reach your desired consistency.
4. If the glaze is too thin, add a bit more powdered sugar, a tablespoon at a time, until you reach your desired consistency.
5. Drizzle the glaze over cooled cakes, cupcakes, or pastries.
6. Allow the glaze to set for a few minutes before serving.

Chocolate Ganache

Ingredients

- 8 oz (225 grams) high-quality dark chocolate, finely chopped
- 1 cup (240 ml) heavy cream

Directions

1. Make sure all ingredients are measured.

2. Prepare the Chocolate: Place the finely chopped dark chocolate in a heatproof bowl. Ensure the chocolate pieces are as uniform as possible for even melting.

3. Heat the Cream: In a small saucepan, heat the heavy cream over medium heat until it just begins to simmer. Do not let it come to a full boil. Tiny bubbles should form around the edges of the pan.

4. Combine Cream and Chocolate: Pour the hot cream over the chopped dark chocolate. Let it sit undisturbed for 2-3 minutes to allow the chocolate to soften and begin melting.

5. Stir Until Smooth: Gently stir the cream and dark chocolate together with a silicone spatula or a whisk until the mixture is completely smooth and glossy. Start from the center and

work your way outward in small circles to ensure thorough mixing.

6. Cool and Use: Allow the ganache to cool slightly before using it as a glaze or filling. If used as a frosting or whipped filling, let it cool at room temperature until it thickens to a spreadable consistency, or refrigerate it for about 30 minutes, stirring occasionally to maintain a smooth texture.

Notes:

o For a Glaze: Use the ganache while it's still warm and pourable. Pour it over cakes, cupcakes, or pastries for a smooth, shiny finish.

o For a Filling: Let the ganache cool to room temperature and thicken slightly before using it to fill cakes, tarts, or pastries.

o For Whipped Ganache: Chill the ganache in the refrigerator until firm, then whip with a hand mixer until light and fluffy. Use as a frosting or filling for cakes and cupcakes.

White Chocolate Ganache

Ingredients

- 8 oz (225 grams) high-quality white chocolate, finely chopped
- 1/2 cup (120 ml) heavy cream

Directions

1. Make sure all ingredients are measured.

2. Prepare the White Chocolate: Place the finely chopped white chocolate in a heatproof bowl. Ensure the chocolate pieces are as uniform as possible for even melting.

3. Heat the Cream: In a small saucepan, heat the heavy cream over medium heat until it just begins to simmer. Do not let it come to a full boil. Tiny bubbles should form around the edges of the pan.

4. Combine Cream and White Chocolate: Pour the hot cream over the chopped white chocolate. Let it sit undisturbed for 2-3 minutes to allow the chocolate to soften and begin melting.

5. Stir Until Smooth: Gently stir the cream and white chocolate together with a silicone spatula or a whisk until the mixture

is completely smooth and glossy. Start from the center and work your way outward in small circles to ensure thorough mixing.

6. Cool and Use: Allow the ganache to cool slightly before using it as a glaze or filling. If using as a frosting or whipped filling, let it cool at room temperature until it thickens to a spreadable consistency, or refrigerate it for about 30 minutes, stirring occasionally to maintain a smooth texture.

Notes:

o For a Glaze: Use the ganache while it's still warm and pourable. Pour it over cakes, cupcakes, or pastries for a smooth, shiny finish.

o For a Filling: Let the ganache cool to room temperature and thicken slightly before using it to fill cakes, tarts, or pastries.

o For Whipped Ganache: Chill the ganache in the refrigerator until firm, then whip with a hand mixer until light and fluffy. Use as a frosting or filling for cakes and cupcakes.

Royal Icing

Ingredients

- 3 large egg whites
- 4 cups powdered sugar (confectioners' sugar)
- 1 tsp vanilla extract
- Food coloring (optional)

Directions

1. Make sure all ingredients are measured.

2. In a clean, grease-free mixing bowl, beat the egg whites until frothy using an electric mixer on medium speed.

3. Gradually add the powdered sugar, one cup at a time, while continuing to beat the mixture on low speed. Scrape down the sides of the bowl as needed.

4. Once all the powdered sugar is incorporated, increase the mixer speed to high and continue beating until the icing forms stiff peaks. This may take about 5-7 minutes.

5. Add the vanilla extract and beat for an additional minute to incorporate.

6. If desired, divide the icing into separate bowls and add food coloring to achieve your desired shades.

7. Transfer the royal icing to piping bags fitted with tips or use a spoon to drizzle it over cookies, cakes, or other treats.

8. Allow the icing to set and harden before serving or decorating further.

Simple Syrup

Ingredients

- 1 cup granulated sugar
- 1 cup water
- Flavoring of your choice (such as vanilla extract, citrus zest, flavored extracts, etc.)

Directions

1. Make sure all ingredients are measured.
2. In a small saucepan, combine the granulated sugar and water.
3. Heat the mixture over medium heat, stirring occasionally, until the sugar is completely dissolved.
4. Once the sugar is dissolved, bring the mixture to a gentle boil.
5. Reduce the heat to low and simmer the syrup for about 5 minutes, stirring occasionally.
6. Remove the saucepan from the heat and let the syrup cool slightly.

7. Stir in your desired flavoring, such as vanilla extract or citrus zest, to infuse the syrup with additional flavor. You can adjust the amount of flavoring to taste.

8. Allow the syrup to cool completely before using.

9. Once cooled, transfer the syrup to a clean bottle or jar with a lid for storage.

To use the simple syrup on cakes:

o   After baking and cooling your cake layers, use a pastry brush to generously brush the simple syrup over the top of each layer.

o   Allow the syrup to soak into the cake layers for a few minutes before assembling and frosting your cake.

You can also use the simple syrup to moisten leftover cake slices or to revive dry cakes.

This simple syrup is versatile and can be customized with different flavorings to complement your cakes. Enjoy!

CHAPTER 3: COOKIES

(Tangela Blackmon; left and Tia; right at the Mervo bakeshop.)

I remember the warm, comforting aroma that filled my grandmother's kitchen whenever she made cookies when I was a child. It was a ritual that I eagerly awaited each time I visited her. I would sit on a stool next to her, watching with wide eyes as she effortlessly mixed the ingredients together.

She would always involve me in the process, letting me help pour flour or crack eggs, even if I made a mess.

As I grew older, I found myself longing to recreate those moments of joy. In the 10th grade, I had the opportunity to do just that in the bake shop at Mergenthaler Vocational Technical Senior High School. I rolled up my sleeves and started to make chocolate chip cookies. It was a breeze. I knew exactly what to do because of my time with my grandmother.

As I baked, I felt a sense of connection to her. When the cookies were done, and I pulled them out of the oven, seeing them golden brown and delicious, I couldn't help but smile. I whispered to myself, "For you, Grandma."

My grandmother would always make cookies for community bake sales. It was her way of giving back. She was well known as the go-to baker to buy the most delicious treats from. I would always assist her when she did bake sales. I loved the hustle and bustle of it all. Setting up the stalls, marketing our treats, and counting the cash.

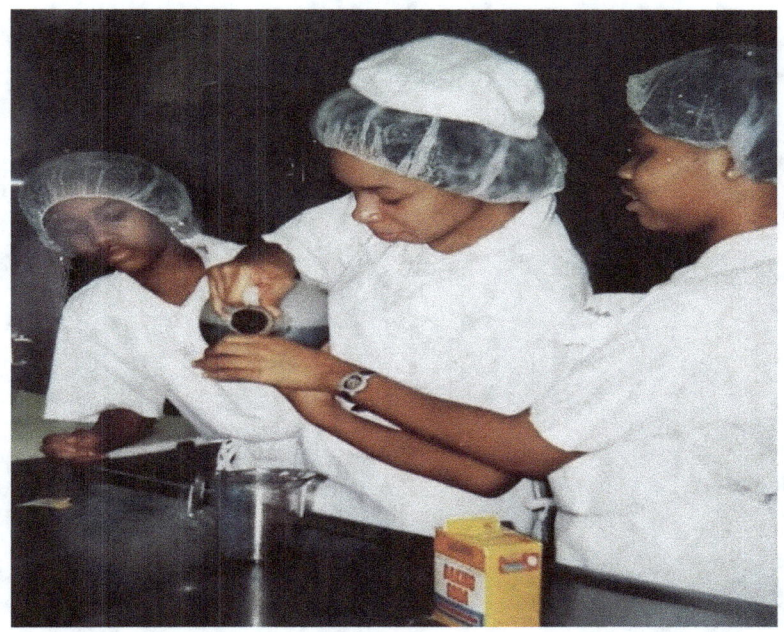

(Tia, left; Precious Jordan, middle; Tangela Blackmon, right. Weighing ingredients to make chocolate chip cookies.)

Those moments with my grandmother taught me valuable lessons about hard work, entrepreneurship, and the joy of sharing something you've created with others. As I took the cookies I baked in class to my peers, I thanked her for teaching me so well.

Chocolate Chip Cookies

Ingredients

- 1 cup (2 sticks) unsalted butter, melted and cooled slightly
- 1 cup granulated sugar
- 1 cup packed light brown sugar
- 2 large eggs
- 2 tsp vanilla extract
- 3 cups all-purpose flour
- 1 teaspoon baking soda
- 1/2 tsp salt
- 2 cups semi-sweet chocolate chunks or chips
- 1 cup chopped walnuts or pecans (optional)

Directions

1. Make sure all ingredients are measured.
2. Turn oven to 350°F. Line baking sheets with parchment paper or silicone baking mats.

3. In a large mixing bowl, whisk together the melted butter, granulated sugar, and brown sugar until well combined.

4. Beat in the eggs one at a time, then add the vanilla extract and mix until smooth.

5. In a separate bowl, sift together the all-purpose flour, baking soda, and salt.

6. Gradually add the dry ingredients to the wet mixture, stirring until just combined.

7. Fold in the chocolate chunks and chopped nuts (if using) until evenly distributed throughout the dough.

8. Using a cookie scoop or spoon, drop rounded tablespoons of dough onto the prepared baking sheets, leaving space between each cookie to allow for spreading.

9. Flatten each cookie slightly with the back of a spoon or your fingers to help them spread evenly while baking.

10. Bake the cookies in the preheated oven for 12-15 minutes or until the edges are golden brown and the tops are set.

11. Allow the cookies to cool on the baking sheets for a few minutes before transferring them to a wire rack to cool completely.

Sugar Cookies

Ingredients

- 1 cup (2 sticks) unsalted butter, softened
- 1 cup granulated sugar
- 1 large egg
- 1 tsp vanilla extract
- 2 1/2 cups all-purpose flour
- 1 tsp baking powder
- 1/2 tsp salt

For Decorating (optional):

- Royal icing
- Sprinkles or colored sugar

Directions

1. Make sure all ingredients are measured.
2. Turn oven to 375°F (190°C). Line baking sheets with parchment paper or silicone baking mats.

3. In a large mixing bowl, cream together the softened butter and granulated sugar until light and fluffy.

4. Beat in the egg and vanilla extract until well combined.

5. In a separate bowl, sift together the all-purpose flour, baking powder, and salt.

6. Gradually add the dry ingredients to the wet mixture, mixing until a smooth dough forms.

7. Divide the dough in half and shape each half into a disk. Wrap each disk in plastic wrap and chill in the refrigerator for at least 1 hour or until firm.

8. Once chilled, remove the dough from the refrigerator and let it sit at room temperature for a few minutes to soften slightly.

9. On a lightly floured surface, roll out the dough to about 1/4-inch thickness. Use cookie cutters to cut out shapes and transfer them to the prepared baking sheets.

10. Place the baking sheets in the preheated oven and bake the cookies for 8-10 minutes or until the edges are lightly golden brown.

11. Allow the cookies to cool on the baking sheets for a few minutes before transferring them to a wire rack to cool completely.

Once cooled, decorate the cookies with royal icing and sprinkles or colored sugar, if desired. Allow the icing to set before serving or storing the cookies in an airtight container.

Veronica's Oatmeal Cookies

Ingredients

- 1 cup (2 sticks) unsalted butter, softened
- 1 cup brown sugar, packed
- 1/2 cup granulated sugar
- 2 large eggs
- 1 tsp vanilla extract
- 1 1/2 cups all-purpose flour
- 1 tsp baking soda
- 1 tsp ground cinnamon
- 1/2 tsp salt
- 3 cups old-fashioned oats
- 1 cup mix-ins (such as chocolate chips, dried cranberries, chopped nuts)

Directions

1. Make sure all ingredients are measured.

2. Turn oven to 350°F (175°C). Line baking sheets with parchment paper or silicone baking mats.

3. In a large mixing bowl, cream together the softened butter, brown sugar, and granulated sugar until light and fluffy.

4. Beat in the eggs one at a time, then add the vanilla extract and mix until well combined.

5. In a separate bowl, whisk together the all-purpose flour, baking soda, ground cinnamon, and salt.

6. Gradually add the dry ingredients to the wet mixture, mixing until just combined.

7. Fold in the old-fashioned oats until evenly distributed throughout the dough.

8. Stir in your choice of mix-ins, such as chocolate chips, dried cranberries, or chopped nuts, until well incorporated.

9. Using a cookie scoop or spoon, drop rounded tablespoons of dough onto the prepared baking sheets, leaving space between each cookie to allow for spreading.

10. Flatten each cookie slightly with the back of a spoon or your fingers to help them spread evenly while baking.

11. Bake the cookies in the preheated oven for 10-12 minutes or until the edges are golden brown and the tops are set.

12. Allow the cookies to cool on the baking sheets for a few minutes before transferring them to a wire rack to cool completely.

(Grandma Veronica, standing outside where she used to sell her baked goods.)

Snickerdoodles

Ingredients

- 1 cup (2 sticks) unsalted butter, softened
- 1 1/2 cups granulated sugar
- 2 large eggs
- 1 tsp vanilla extract
- 3 cups all-purpose flour
- 2 tsp cream of tartar
- 1 tsp baking soda
- 1/2 tsp salt
- 2 Tbsp ground cinnamon

For Rolling:

- 1/4 cup granulated sugar
- 1 Tbsp ground cinnamon

Directions

1. Make sure all ingredients are measured.

2. Turn oven to 350°F. Line baking sheets with parchment paper or silicone baking mats.

3. In a large mixing bowl, cream together the softened butter and 1 1/2 cups of granulated sugar until light and fluffy.

4. Beat in the eggs one at a time, then add the vanilla extract and mix until well combined.

5. In a separate bowl, whisk together the all-purpose flour, cream of tartar, baking soda, salt, and 2 tablespoons of ground cinnamon.

6. Gradually add the dry ingredients to the wet mixture, mixing until just combined.

7. In a small bowl, mix the remaining 1/4 cup of granulated sugar and 1 tablespoon of ground cinnamon for rolling.

8. Scoop out portions of dough and roll them into balls about 1 inch in diameter.

9. Roll each dough ball in the cinnamon-sugar mixture until evenly coated.

10. Place the coated dough balls onto the prepared baking sheets, leaving space between each one to allow for spreading.

11. Flatten each cookie slightly with the bottom of a glass or your fingers to help them spread evenly while baking.

12. Bake the cookies in the preheated oven for 8-10 minutes or until the edges are set and the tops are lightly golden brown.

Allow the cookies to cool on the baking sheets for a few minutes before transferring them to a wire rack to cool completely.

"Making Cookies Motivation Time"

"Let's talk about making cookies. Not just any cookies, but those homemade, straight-from-the-heart kind. You know, the ones you think about days later.

There's something truly lovely about the whole process of making it all come together. It's not always perfect, and that's the beauty of it. Sometimes, you'll make a mess, and the cookies won't turn out as planned, but it's all part of the experience.

Every time you bake for others, there's a sense of connection. Maybe it's memories of baking with loved ones or the anticipation of sharing something delicious with friends. Whatever it is, it's real.

So, as you mix, scoop, and bake, remember you're not just making cookies. You're creating moments. Moments of laughter, comfort, and love. And in a world that can often feel chaotic, those moments are everything.

Keep on baking, keep on sharing.

You got this."

– Shatia Godfrey

Peanut Butter Cookies

Ingredients

- 1 cup creamy or chunky peanut butter
- 1/2 cup unsalted butter, softened
- 1/2 cup granulated sugar
- 1/2 cup brown sugar, packed
- 1 large egg
- 1 1/4 cups all-purpose flour
- 1 tsp baking soda
- 1/2 tsp baking powder
- 1 tsp vanilla extract
- 1/4 tsp salt

Directions

1. Make sure all ingredients are measured.
2. Turn oven to 350°F (175°C). Line a baking sheet with parchment paper or lightly grease it.

3. In a large mixing bowl, cream the creamy or chunky peanut butter, softened butter, granulated sugar, and brown sugar. Mix until light and fluffy.

4. Beat in the egg and vanilla extract until well combined.

5. In a separate bowl, whisk together the flour, baking soda, baking powder, and salt. Gradually add the dry ingredients to the wet mixture and stir until just combined.

6. Roll the dough into 1-inch balls and place them on the prepared baking sheet. Use a fork to press down gently on each ball, creating a crisscross pattern.

7. Bake the cookies in the preheated oven for 10-12 minutes or until the edges are lightly golden brown. The center will still be soft but will firm up as it cools.

8. Allow the cookies to cool on the baking sheet for 15 minutes before transferring them to a wire rack to cool completely.

Lemon Burst Cookies

Ingredients

- 1 cup (2 sticks) unsalted butter, softened
- 1 cup granulated sugar
- 2 large eggs
- Zest of 2 lemons
- 2 Tbsp fresh lemon juice
- 1 tsp vanilla extract
- 3 cups all-purpose flour
- 1 tsp baking powder
- 1/2 tsp baking soda
- 1/4 tsp salt
- 1/2 cup powdered sugar for rolling

Directions

1. Make sure all ingredients are measured.

2. Turn oven to 350°F (175°C). Line baking sheets with parchment paper or silicone baking mats.

3. In a large mixing bowl, cream together the softened butter and granulated sugar until light and fluffy.

4. Beat in the eggs one at a time, then add the lemon zest, lemon juice, and vanilla extract. Mix until well combined.

5. In a separate bowl, sift together the all-purpose flour, baking powder, baking soda, and salt.

6. Gradually add the dry ingredients to the wet mixture, mixing until a smooth dough forms.

7. Place the powdered sugar in a small bowl.

8. Scoop out portions of dough and roll them into balls about 1 inch in diameter.

9. Roll each dough ball in the powdered sugar until evenly coated.

10. Place the coated dough balls onto the prepared baking sheets, leaving space between each one to allow for spreading.

11. Flatten each cookie slightly with the bottom of a glass or your fingers.

12. Bake the cookies in the preheated oven for 10-12 minutes or until the edges are lightly golden brown.

13. Allow the cookies to cool on the baking sheets for 15 minutes before transferring them to a wire rack to cool completely.

White Chocolate Macadamia Cookies

Ingredients

- 1 cup (2 sticks) unsalted butter, softened
- 1 cup brown sugar, packed
- 1/2 cup granulated sugar
- 2 large eggs
- 1 tsp vanilla extract
- 2 1/4 cups all-purpose flour
- 1 tsp baking soda
- 1/2 tsp salt
- 1 cup white chocolate chips
- 1 cup macadamia nuts, roughly chopped

Directions

1. Make sure all ingredients are measured.
2. Turn oven to 350°F (175°C). Line a baking sheet with parchment paper or lightly grease it.

3. In a large mixing bowl, cream together the softened butter, brown sugar, and granulated sugar until smooth and creamy.

4. Add the eggs, one at a time, mixing well after each addition. Stir in the vanilla extract until combined.

5. In a separate bowl, whisk together the all-purpose flour, baking soda, and salt.

6. Gradually add the dry ingredients to the wet ingredients, mixing until just combined.

7. Fold in the white chocolate chips and chopped macadamia nuts until evenly distributed throughout the dough.

8. Using a cookie scoop or spoon, drop rounded tablespoons of dough onto the prepared baking sheet, spacing them about 2 inches apart.

9. Bake in the preheated oven for 10-12 minutes or until the edges are lightly golden brown.

10. Allow the cookies to cool on the baking sheet for 15 minutes before transferring them to a wire rack to cool completely.

CHAPTER 4: BREAD AND DOUGHNUTS

Sophomore year was the year when we started our baking classes at Mergenthaler Vocational-Technical Senior High School. One of the first baked goods we learned how to make was doughnuts. Mrs. Conigliaro would demonstrate the process, and we would pay close attention.

We would mix the dough in our 60-quart mixer until it was a smooth ball. Then, my favorite part of the doughnut process was kneading the dough and putting it through the dough roller machine. Next, we would cut out the doughnuts and proof them in the proof box. We then learned why we had to proof the dough and for how long.

After the doughnuts doubled in size, it was time to fry the doughnut until golden brown. Our glaze team then glazed the doughnuts at the glazing table.

Bakeshop doughnuts we're true perfection. Mrs. Conigliaro would allow us to have a doughnut on that day. These doughnuts were warm, mouth-watering, and melted in your mouth. If you know, you know. After all the doughnuts were fried and glazed, our class would take them down to the cafeteria and sell them to the school for $.50.

The humming of the baking equipment and the lessons learned always brought satisfaction to my day. Bakeshop didn't feel like work; it was my sanctuary.

- Shatia Godfrey

Doughnuts

Ingredients

- 1 cup whole milk, warmed to about 110°F (43°C)
- 2 1/4 tsp (1 packet) active dry yeast
- 1/3 cup granulated sugar
- 2 large eggs
- 1/2 cup (1 stick) unsalted butter, melted and cooled slightly
- 4 cups all-purpose flour, plus extra for dusting
- 1/2 tsp salt
- Oil, for frying
- Doughnut topping (vanilla glaze, powdered sugar, cinnamon sugar, etc.)

Paired well with Vanilla Glaze, Chapter 2

Directions

1. Make sure all ingredients are measured.

2. In a small bowl, combine the warm milk and active dry yeast. Let it sit for about 5-10 minutes until frothy.

3. In a large mixing bowl or the bowl of a stand mixer fitted with a dough hook, combine the frothy yeast mixture with the sugar, eggs, and melted butter. Mix until well combined.

4. Gradually add the flour and salt to the wet ingredients, mixing until a soft dough forms. If using a stand mixer, knead the dough on medium speed for about 5-7 minutes. If kneading by hand, turn the dough out onto a lightly floured surface and knead for about 8-10 minutes until smooth and elastic.

5. Place the dough in a lightly greased bowl, cover it with plastic wrap or a clean kitchen towel, and let it rise in a warm, draft-free place for about 1-1.5 hours or until doubled in size.

6. Once the dough has risen, punch it down gently to deflate it, then turn it out onto a lightly floured surface. Roll the dough out to about 1/2-inch thickness.

7. Using a doughnut cutter or two round cutters (one larger and one smaller for the center hole), cut out doughnuts and place them on a lightly floured baking sheet. Gather any scraps of dough, re-roll, and cut out more doughnuts.

8. Cover the cut doughnuts with a clean kitchen towel and let them rise again for about 30-45 minutes or until puffy.

9. While the doughnuts are rising, heat oil in a large pot or deep fryer to 350°F (175°C).

10. Carefully add the risen doughnuts to the hot oil, a few at a time, being careful not to overcrowd the pot. Fry each side for about 1-2 minutes or until golden brown.

11. Remove the fried doughnuts from the oil using a slotted spoon and place them on a wire rack lined with paper towels to drain excess oil.

12. Allow the doughnuts to cool slightly before glazing or coating with your favorite toppings. Enjoy these classic yeast-raised doughnuts warm or at room temperature!

Quick Rolls

Ingredients

- 2 1/4 cups all-purpose flour
- 1 Tbsp sugar
- 1 tsp salt
- 1 Tbsp instant yeast
- 1 cup warm water
- 2 Tbsp melted butter
- Additional melted butter for brushing

Directions

1. Make sure all ingredients are measured.
2. Turn oven to 375°F (190°C). Lightly grease a baking sheet or line it with parchment paper.
3. In a large mixing bowl, combine the flour, sugar, salt, and instant yeast.
4. Add the warm water and melted butter to the dry ingredients. Mix until a soft dough forms.

5. Turn the dough out onto a lightly floured surface and knead for about 5 minutes until the dough is smooth and elastic.

6. Divide the dough into 12 equal pieces and shape each piece into a ball.

7. Place the dough balls on the prepared baking sheet, leaving a little space between each one.

8. Cover the rolls with a clean kitchen towel and let them rise in a warm place for about 15-20 minutes or until slightly puffy.

9. Once risen, brush the tops of the rolls with melted butter.

10. Bake in the preheated oven for 12-15 minutes or until the rolls are golden brown on top and sound hollow when tapped on the bottom.

11. Remove from the oven and let cool slightly before serving.

Raisin Bread

Ingredients

- 1 cup warm milk (about 110°F/45°C)
- 2 1/4 tsp (1 packet) active dry yeast
- 3 cups all-purpose flour, divided
- 1 tsp salt
- 2 Tbsp unsalted butter, melted
- 1/4 cup granulated sugar
- 1 cup raisins
- 1 egg, beaten (for egg wash)
- 1 Tbsp milk (for egg wash)

Directions

1. Make sure all ingredients are measured.
2. In a small bowl, combine the warm milk and active dry yeast. Let it sit for about 5 minutes until foamy.

3. In a large mixing bowl or the bowl of a stand mixer fitted with the dough hook attachment, combine 2 cups of flour and salt.

4. Add the melted butter and granulated sugar to the flour mixture. Pour in the activated yeast mixture as well.

5. Stir until well combined, then gradually add the remaining cup of flour, 1/2 cup at a time, until a soft dough forms.

6. Turn the dough out onto a lightly floured surface and knead for about 5-7 minutes until smooth and elastic.

7. Place the dough in a greased bowl, cover it with a clean kitchen towel or plastic wrap, and let it rise in a warm place for about 1-1.5 hours or until doubled in size.

8. Once the dough has risen, punch it down and turn it out onto a lightly floured surface. Flatten it into a rectangle about 1/2 inch thick.

9. Sprinkle the raisins evenly over the surface of the dough. Roll the dough up tightly, jelly-roll style, starting from one of the long sides.

10. Pinch the seams and ends to seal and place the rolled dough seam side down in a greased loaf pan.

11. Cover the loaf pan with a clean kitchen towel and let the dough rise for another 30-45 minutes until puffy.

12. Turn oven to 350°F (175°C).

13. In a small bowl, whisk together the beaten egg and a tablespoon of milk to make an egg wash. Brush the top of the risen dough with the egg wash.

14. Bake the bread in the preheated oven for 30-35 minutes or until golden brown on top and sounds hollow when tapped on the bottom.

15. Remove the bread from the oven and let it cool in the pan for 10 minutes. Then, transfer the loaf to a wire rack to cool completely before slicing.

16. Once cooled, slice and serve.

"Making Bread Motivation Time"

"There's satisfaction when it comes to creating dough: combining all the ingredients in the mixing bowl and watching it twirl together with the dough hook. And when the mixing is done, putting your hand on the cold and smooth dough is a true reward. My favorite part is kneading and shaping the dough into the desired shape.

Beyond the magic of the bread-making process, there can be a sense of anxiousness, hoping that the dough rises during the proofing stage or did I follow the recipe spot on. Creating dough can also remind us of how life can be at times. Sure, there may be bumps and lumps, but as time goes on, and if we practice a little patience, life will smooth out.

Don't worry about mishaps and mistakes- they happen. Have fun! Embrace the rhythm of kneading the cool dough and how your hands feel when they are dusted with flour. When you fold the dough by kneading, slow down and pay attention to the motions and the comfort the bread-making process brings to your soul. Trust yourself; you have the power to make something special from flour, eggs, and butter. Let your hands guide you, and let the aroma of fresh bread fill your kitchen. You got this!"

– Shatia Godfrey

White Bread

Ingredients

- 1 cup warm water (about 110°F/45°C)
- 2 1/4 tsp (1 packet) active dry yeast
- 2 Tbsp granulated sugar
- 1 cup milk, warmed
- 2 Tbsp unsalted butter, melted
- 1 Tbsp salt
- 5-6 cups all-purpose flour

Directions

1. Make sure all ingredients are measured.

2. In a small bowl, combine the warm water, active dry yeast, and granulated sugar. Stir gently and let it sit for about 5 minutes until foamy.

3. In a large mixing bowl or the bowl of a stand mixer fitted with the dough hook attachment, combine the warm milk, melted butter, and salt.

4. Add the yeast mixture to the milk mixture and stir until well combined.

5. Gradually add the flour, 1 cup at a time, mixing well after each addition until a soft dough forms. The dough should come together and pull away from the sides of the bowl.

6. Turn the dough out onto a lightly floured surface and knead for about 5-7 minutes until smooth and elastic. If using a stand mixer, knead the dough on medium speed for the same amount of time.

7. Place the dough in a greased bowl, cover it with a clean kitchen towel or plastic wrap, and let it rise in a warm place for about 1-1.5 hours or until doubled in size.

8. Once the dough has risen, punch it down and divide it into two equal portions.

9. Shape each portion into a loaf and place them in greased 9x5-inch loaf pans.

10. Cover the loaf pans with a clean kitchen towel and let the dough rise for another 30-45 minutes until puffy.

11. Turn oven to 375°F (190°C).

12. Bake the loaves in the preheated oven for 25-30 minutes or until golden brown on top and sounds hollow when tapped on the bottom.

13. Remove the bread from the oven and let it cool in the pans for 5 minutes. Then, transfer the loaves to a wire rack to cool completely before slicing.

14. Once cooled, slice and serve.

Buttermilk Biscuits

Ingredients

- 2 cups all-purpose flour
- 1 Tbsp baking powder
- 1/2 tsp baking soda
- 1 tsp salt
- 1/4 cup unsalted butter, cold and cubed
- 3/4 cup buttermilk, cold

Directions

1. Make sure all ingredients are measured.

2. Turn oven to 425°F (220°C). Line a baking sheet with parchment paper or lightly grease it.

3. In a large mixing bowl, whisk together the flour, baking powder, baking soda, and salt until well combined.

4. Add the cold, cubed butter to the dry ingredients. Use a pastry cutter or your fingers to cut the butter into the flour mixture until it resembles coarse crumbs.

5. Make a well in the center of the mixture and pour in the cold buttermilk.

6. Using a fork or a wooden spoon, gently stir the mixture until it just comes together into a shaggy dough. Be careful not to overmix.

7. Turn the dough out onto a lightly floured surface. Gently knead it a few times until it forms a cohesive ball but be careful not to overwork the dough.

8. Pat the dough out into a circle or rectangle that's about 1 inch thick.

9. Use a floured biscuit cutter or the rim of a glass to cut out biscuits. Press straight down without twisting the cutter to ensure the biscuits rise evenly.

10. Place the biscuits on the prepared baking sheet, leaving a little space between each one.

11. Gather any remaining dough scraps, gently pat them together, and cut out more biscuits until all the dough is used.

12. Bake the biscuits in the preheated oven for 12-15 minutes or until they are golden brown on top and cooked through.

13. Remove from the oven and let the biscuits cool slightly on the baking sheet before serving.

Banana Bread

Ingredients

- 3 ripe bananas, mashed
- 1/2 cup (1 stick) unsalted butter, melted
- 1/2 cup brown sugar
- 1/4 cup granulated sugar
- 2 large eggs
- 1 tsp vanilla extract
- 1 3/4 cups all-purpose flour
- 1 tsp baking powder
- 1/2 tsp baking soda
- 1/2 tsp salt
- 1 tsp ground cinnamon
- 1/4 tsp ground nutmeg
- 1/2 cup chopped walnuts or pecans (optional)

Directions

1. Make sure all ingredients are measured.

2. Turn oven to 350°F (175°C). Grease a 9x5-inch loaf pan or line it with parchment paper.

3. In a large mixing bowl, mash the ripe bananas until smooth.

4. Add the melted butter, brown sugar, and granulated sugar to the mashed bananas. Mix well until combined.

5. Beat in the eggs, one at a time, until fully incorporated. Stir in the vanilla extract.

6. In a separate bowl, whisk together the flour, baking powder, baking soda, salt, cinnamon, and nutmeg.

7. Gradually add the dry ingredients to the wet ingredients, mixing until just combined. Be careful not to overmix.

8. If using, fold in the chopped walnuts or pecans until evenly distributed throughout the batter.

9. Pour the batter into the prepared loaf pan and spread it out evenly.

10. Bake in the preheated oven for 50-60 minutes or until a toothpick inserted into the center comes out clean.

11. Allow the banana bread to cool in the pan for 10-15 minutes before transferring it to a wire rack to cool completely.

12. Once cooled, slice and serve.

Pie Crust

Ingredients

- 1 1/4 cups all-purpose flour
- 1/2 tsp salt
- 1/2 tsp granulated sugar
- 1/2 cup (1 stick) unsalted butter, cold and cut into small cubes
- 2-4 Tbsp ice water

Directions

1. Make sure all ingredients are measured.
2. In a large mixing bowl, combine the flour, granulated sugar and salt.
3. Add the cold cubed butter to the flour mixture.
4. Use a pastry cutter or your fingers to cut the butter into the flour until the mixture resembles coarse crumbs with some pea-sized pieces of butter remaining.
5. Gradually add the ice water, 1 tablespoon at a time, mixing gently with a fork or your hands just until the dough begins to come together. Be careful not to overwork the dough.

6. Once the dough starts to hold together, shape it into a ball and flatten it into a disk.

7. Wrap the dough in plastic wrap and refrigerate for at least 30 minutes (or up to 2 days) before using.

8. When ready to use, remove the dough from the refrigerator and let it sit at room temperature for a few minutes to slightly soften.

9. On a lightly floured surface, roll out the dough into a circle about 12 inches in diameter, depending on the size of your pie dish.

10. Carefully transfer the rolled-out dough to your pie dish, pressing it gently into the bottom and sides.

11. Trim any excess dough hanging over the edges of the pie dish and crimp the edges as desired.

12. Follow the instructions for your pie recipe, whether it requires a pre-baked crust or a filling to be added directly to the unbaked crust.

CHAPTER 5: SPECIALTIES

In the early 2000, I joined Baltimore International College, a culinary arts school with hopes and dreams to one day open a bakery. I was so proud to be the first member of my family to go to college and graduate. I stood there with colleagues who had the same dream: to open a restaurant or a bakery. It was here that I learned how to temper chocolate and create different types of confectioners. I was beginning to refine my craft and take the next steps in my baking career.

When I think about specialty desserts, one memory comes to mind. I was in my classical pastries and desserts class, and our Master Pastry Chef taught us the art of making a perfect crème brûlée. It was now our turn; we meticulously combined the heavy cream, egg yolks, sugar, and vanilla. Creating a soft and creamy texture and carefully torching the sugar that was on the top of the ceramic dishes ensuring that we did not over burn the crispy layer.

Specialty desserts are decadent desserts that require patience and precision. On that day, we created something extraordinary. I was proud that I mastered creating an exquisite dessert, which turned into one of my favorite specialty desserts.

In the years to come, I would continue to create specialty desserts and have them on Tia Sweet Tooth's menu.

Crème Brûlée

Ingredients

- 2 cups heavy cream
- 1/2 cup granulated sugar
- 4 large egg yolks
- 1 tsp vanilla extract
- 1/4 tsp salt
- 4 Tbsp brown sugar for caramelizing

Directions

1. Make sure all ingredients are measured.
2. Turn oven to 325°F (160°C). Place six ramekins in a baking dish and set aside.
3. In a saucepan, heat the heavy cream over medium heat until it just begins to simmer. Remove from heat and let it cool slightly.
4. In a mixing bowl, whisk together the granulated sugar, egg yolks, vanilla extract, and salt until well combined.

5. Slowly pour the warm cream into the egg mixture, whisking constantly to prevent curdling.

6. Strain the mixture through a fine-mesh sieve into a pouring jug to ensure smooth custard.

7. Divide the custard evenly among the ramekins.

8. Fill the baking dish with hot water halfway up the sides of the ramekins to create a water bath.

9. Carefully transfer the baking dish to the preheated oven and bake for 35-40 minutes, or until the custards are set around the edges but still slightly jiggly in the center.

10. Remove the ramekins from the water bath and let them cool to room temperature. Then, refrigerate them for at least 2 hours or overnight until fully chilled and set.

11. Once chilled, evenly sprinkle a thin layer of brown sugar over the top of each custard.

12. Using a kitchen torch, carefully caramelize the sugar until it forms a golden-brown crust.

13. Allow the caramelized sugar to harden for a minute before serving.

Banana Pudding

Ingredients

- 3 large ripe bananas, sliced
- 1 box of vanilla wafers or 2 boxes of Chessman Cookies
- 2 cups whole milk
- 1 cup heavy cream
- 1/2 cup granulated sugar
- 1/4 cup cornstarch
- 4 large egg yolks
- 1 tsp vanilla extract
- 1/4 tsp salt

Directions

1. Make sure all ingredients are measured.
2. In a medium saucepan, combine the whole milk and heavy cream over medium heat. Heat until just simmering, then remove from heat and set aside.

3. In a separate bowl, whisk together the granulated sugar, cornstarch, egg yolks, vanilla extract, and salt until smooth and well combined.

4. Gradually pour the warm milk mixture into the egg yolk mixture, whisking constantly to prevent scrambling the eggs.

5. Return the mixture to the saucepan and place it back over medium heat. Cook, stirring constantly, until the pudding thickens and coats the back of a spoon, about 5-7 minutes.

6. Remove the pudding from heat and let it cool slightly.

7. In a large trifle dish or individual serving cups, layer the vanilla wafers, sliced bananas, and pudding, starting with a layer of pudding at the bottom.

8. Continue layering until all ingredients are used, ending with a layer of pudding on top.

9. Cover the dish with plastic wrap and refrigerate for at least 2 hours or until the pudding is set and chilled.

Before serving, garnish with additional banana slices and crushed vanilla wafers or Chessman cookies if desired.

Candy Apples

Ingredients

- 6 medium-sized apples (Granny Smith or Honeycrisp work well)
- 2 cups granulated sugar
- 1 cup light corn syrup
- 1/2 cup water
- 1 tsp vanilla extract or your favorite flavor
- Food coloring (gel or liquid), as desired

Directions

1. Make sure all ingredients are measured.
2. Wash and dry the apples thoroughly. Remove the stems and insert wooden sticks or skewers into the stem end of each apple. Place them on a parchment-lined baking sheet and set aside.
3. In a medium saucepan, combine the granulated sugar, corn syrup, and water. Stir over medium heat until the sugar dissolves.

4. Once the mixture comes to a boil, insert a candy thermometer into the saucepan and cook without stirring until it reaches 300°F (hard crack stage), about 10-15 minutes.

5. Remove the saucepan from heat and stir in the vanilla extract or desired flavor. If using food coloring, add a few drops of food coloring. Stir until the desired color is achieved.

6. Working quickly but carefully, dip each apple into the colored sugar syrup mixture, tilting the saucepan as needed to coat the entire apple. Allow any excess syrup to drip off.

7. Place the coated apples back onto the parchment-lined baking sheet and allow them to cool and harden completely at room temperature. This may take about 30 minutes to an hour.

Once the sugar glaze has set and the apples have cooled, your classic candy apples are ready to enjoy!

To clean the saucepan, add water, place it back on the stove, and let it boil. Once the leftover sugar has dissolved, empty it into the sink.

"Making Specialties Motivation Time"

"Specialty cakes and desserts are elaborate treats that allow you to be creative and experiment with different methods and flavors. These show stoppers are not your typical chocolate cake or sweet potato pie. They burst with flavor, texture, and great presentation.

When you begin to delve into creating specialty desserts, you open up new techniques that will refine your skill as a baker. Your dessert catalog will expand, and everyone who encounters your delectables will fall in love.

Beyond the technical aspect of crafting these specialty treats, they unlock sweet memories and pure joy. Perfection is not the key at first when making specialty desserts like macarons or frozen souffle; it's the enjoyment of doing something you love. Each creation is your sign of love, and sharing your love around is influential.

As we move forward with creating specialty desserts, let's understand that we're not just baking enthusiasts; we're enthused by what we bake. There's happiness in creating something we put our all into and giving it to the ones we love. It's about the smiles, joy, warmth, memories, and fellowship that make all the difference. You create sweet treats because your creativity knows no bounds. In fact, the sky isn't the limit; you are. You got this!"

– Shatia Godfrey

Rice Crispy Treats

Ingredients

- 6 cups crispy rice cereal
- 1/4 cup unsalted butter
- 1 package (10 oz) marshmallows
- 1 tsp vanilla extract
- 1/2 cup mini chocolate chips (optional)
- 1/2 cup chopped toasted nuts (such as almonds or pecans) (optional)
- 1/4 tsp salt (optional)

Directions

1. Make sure all ingredients are measured.

2. Grease a 9x13-inch baking pan with butter or line it with parchment paper.

3. In a large pot, melt the butter over medium heat. Add the marshmallows and stir continuously until they are completely melted and smooth.

4. Remove the pot from the heat and stir in the vanilla extract. If desired, add a pinch of salt for flavor enhancement.

5. Quickly add the crispy rice cereal to the marshmallow mixture and gently fold until the cereal is evenly coated.

6. If using, fold in the optional mini chocolate chips and/or chopped nuts until they are evenly distributed throughout the mixture.

Transfer the mixture to the prepared baking pan and use a spatula or greased hands to press it firmly and evenly into the pan.

Allow the Rice Krispies Treats to cool at room temperature for about 30 minutes or until they are set.

Chocolate-Covered Strawberries

Ingredients

- 1 lb. fresh strawberries, rinsed and dried thoroughly
- 8 oz high-quality dark chocolate, chopped (or chocolate chips)
- 4 oz white chocolate, chopped (optional for drizzling)
- Assorted toppings for decorating (e.g., chopped nuts, shredded coconut, sprinkles, crushed cookies)

Directions

1. Make sure all ingredients are measured.
2. Line a baking sheet with parchment paper or wax paper.
3. In a heatproof bowl set over a pot of simmering water (double boiler), melt the dark chocolate, stirring occasionally until smooth and completely melted.
4. Once the chocolate is melted, remove the bowl from the heat.
5. Holding each strawberry by the stem, dip it into the melted chocolate, swirling to coat evenly. Allow any excess chocolate to drip back into the bowl.

6. Place the chocolate-covered strawberries onto the prepared baking sheet.

7. If desired, sprinkle the strawberries with your choice of toppings while the chocolate is still wet. Get creative with different combinations of nuts, coconut, sprinkles, or crushed cookies.

8. Repeat the dipping and decorating process with the remaining strawberries.

9. If using white chocolate for drizzling, melt it using the same method as the dark chocolate. Transfer the melted white chocolate to a piping bag or a zip-top bag with a small corner snipped off.

10. Drizzle the melted white chocolate over the chocolate-covered strawberries in a zigzag pattern.

11. Allow the chocolate-covered strawberries to set at room temperature until the chocolate hardens or place them in the refrigerator for faster setting.

12. Once the chocolate has set, transfer the strawberries to a serving platter or store them in an airtight container in the refrigerator until ready to serve.

Tiramisu

Ingredients

- 1 cup strong brewed coffee, cooled to room temperature
- 3 Tbsp coffee liqueur (e.g., Kahlua), divided
- 1 cup mascarpone cheese at room temperature
- 1/2 cup powdered sugar
- 1 tsp vanilla extract
- 1 cup heavy cream
- 24 ladyfinger cookies (about 7 ounces)
- Unsweetened cocoa powder for dusting
- Dark chocolate shavings for garnish (optional)

Directions

1. Make sure all ingredients are measured.
2. In a shallow dish, combine the cooled brewed coffee with 2 tablespoons of coffee liqueur. Set aside.

3. In a mixing bowl, beat the mascarpone cheese, powdered sugar, vanilla extract, and remaining tablespoon of coffee liqueur until smooth and creamy.

4. In a separate mixing bowl, whip the heavy cream until stiff peaks form.

5. Gently fold the whipped cream into the mascarpone mixture until well combined and smooth. Set aside.

6. Quickly dip each ladyfinger cookie into the coffee mixture, ensuring it's soaked but not overly soggy.

7. Arrange a layer of soaked ladyfinger cookies in the bottom of an 8x8 inch square dish or a similar-sized serving dish, breaking cookies if necessary to fit.

8. Spread half of the mascarpone mixture evenly over the layer of soaked ladyfinger cookies.

9. Repeat with another layer of soaked ladyfinger cookies and the remaining mascarpone mixture.

10. Cover the dish with plastic wrap and refrigerate for at least 4 hours or overnight to allow the flavors to meld and the tiramisu to set.

11. Before serving, sift a generous dusting of unsweetened cocoa powder over the top of the tiramisu.

12. Optionally, garnish with dark chocolate shavings for an extra touch of decadence.

Slice and serve chilled.

Cheesecake

Ingredients

For the filling:

- 24 oz (about 3 packages) cream cheese, softened
- 1 cup granulated sugar
- 3 large eggs at room temperature
- 1 Tbsp all-purpose flour
- 1 tsp vanilla extract
- Zest of 1 lemon (optional)

For the crust:

- 1 1/2 cups graham cracker crumbs
- 1/4 cup granulated sugar
- 1/2 cup (1 stick) unsalted butter, melted
- **For the topping (optional):**
  Fresh berries, fruit compote, or your favorite topping

Directions

1. Make sure all ingredients are measured.

2. Turn oven to 325°F (160°C). Grease a 9-inch springform pan with butter or non-stick cooking spray.

3. In a mixing bowl, combine the graham cracker crumbs, sugar, and melted butter until well combined.

4. Press the mixture evenly into the bottom of the prepared springform pan, using the back of a spoon or your fingers to pack it tightly.

5. Bake the crust in the preheated oven for 10 minutes. Remove from the oven and let it cool while you prepare the filling.

Make the filling:

1. In a large mixing bowl, beat the softened cream cheese and sugar together until smooth and creamy.

2. Add the eggs one at a time, beating well after each addition.

3. Mix in the flour, vanilla extract, and lemon zest (if using) until well combined and smooth.

Pour the filling over the cooled crust in the springform pan, smoothing the top with a spatula.

Bake the cheesecake:

1. Place the springform pan on a baking sheet (to catch any potential leaks) and bake in the preheated oven for 45-50 minutes, or until the edges are set and the center is slightly jiggly.

2. Turn off the oven, crack the oven door open, and let the cheesecake cool inside the oven for 1 hour.

3. Remove the cheesecake from the oven and let it cool completely at room temperature. Then, cover and refrigerate for at least 4 hours or overnight to chill and set.

Serve:

1. Once chilled and set, carefully remove the sides of the springform pan.

Slice and serve your delicious homemade cheesecake as is or with your favorite toppings such as fresh berries, fruit compote, or whipped cream.

Biscoff Cheesecake

Ingredients

For the filling:

- 24 oz (about 3 packages) cream cheese, softened
- 1 cup Biscoff cookie spread (smooth or crunchy)
- 3/4 cup granulated sugar
- 3 large eggs at room temperature
- 1 tsp vanilla extract
- 1/2 cup heavy whipping cream

For the crust:

- 1 1/2 cups Biscoff cookie crumbs (about 24 cookies)
- 1/4 cup unsalted butter, melted

For the topping:

- 1/4 cup Biscoff cookie spread, warmed slightly for drizzling
- Crushed Biscoff cookies for garnish (optional)

Directions

1. Make sure all ingredients are measured.
2. Turn oven to 325°F (160°C). Grease a 9-inch springform pan with butter or non-stick cooking spray.

Make the crust:

1. Crush the Biscoff cookies in a food processor until they form fine crumbs. Alternatively, you can place the cookies in a zip-top bag and crush them using a rolling pin.
2. In a mixing bowl, combine the Biscoff cookie crumbs and melted butter until well combined.
3. Press the mixture evenly into the bottom of the prepared springform pan, using the back of a spoon or your fingers to pack it tightly.
4. Bake the crust in the preheated oven for 10 minutes. Remove from the oven and let it cool while you prepare the filling.

Make the filling:

1. In a large mixing bowl, beat the softened cream cheese, Biscoff cookie spread, and granulated sugar together until smooth and creamy.
2. Add the eggs one at a time, beating well after each addition.
3. Mix in the vanilla extract until well combined and smooth.
4. In a separate bowl, whip the heavy whipping cream until stiff peaks form.
5. Gently fold the whipped cream into the cream cheese mixture until well combined.
6. Pour the filling over the cooled crust in the springform pan, smoothing the top with a spatula.

Bake the cheesecake:

1. Place the springform pan on a baking sheet (to catch any potential leaks) and bake in the preheated oven for 45-50 minutes, or until the edges are set and the center is slightly jiggly.

2. Turn off the oven, crack the oven door open, and let the cheesecake cool inside the oven for 1 hour.

3. Remove the cheesecake from the oven and let it cool completely at room temperature. Then, cover and refrigerate for at least 4 hours or overnight to chill and set.

Serve:

1. Once chilled and set, carefully remove the sides of the springform pan.

2. Drizzle the warmed Biscoff cookie spread over the top of the cheesecake. If desired, garnish with crushed Biscoff cookies before serving.

CHAPTER 6: PIES

It's official, thanksgiving is not only turkey season, it's also pie season. My grandmother was known for her pies. When I was younger, she would make sweet potato and apple pie, and it was simply perfection. I loved warm pie topped with vanilla ice cream or whipped cream. Inspired by my grandmother's sweet potato pie, I decided to recreate my grandmother's sweet and creamy sweet potato pie for a Friendsgiving one year.

Ready with a recipe online, I began to work in the kitchen. As I peeled and mashed the sweet potatoes, the comforting smell of cinnamon, allspice, and vanilla filled the kitchen. The aroma instantly put me in a happy place; that's when I knew the holidays had begun.

When I started adding the other ingredients, I began to worry. I said to myself what if the pies aren't sweet and creamy? What if no one enjoys it? And more importantly, what if the sweet potato pie doesn't taste like Grandma's? Powering through the recipe that I found online, I told myself that it's ok if it doesn't come out quite as good as your grandmother's sweet potato pie. You put your heart into it!

After my family and friends ate their delicious meals, it was now dessert time. I held my breath as our guest started slicing the sweet potato pie. I watched facial expressions, and their faces were filled with delight. My grandmother may not have passed down the recipe, but the recipe was good enough for me to start the tradition.

As we gathered around the dinner table, sharing memorable moments and eating our sweet potato pie, I realized that this wasn't about whether the pie came out right. Thanksgiving was about laughter, unity, and trying new things. Reflecting back, I can see all of the smiles, and I can still feel the joy everyone had just being with loved ones.

Sweet Potato Pie

Ingredients

- 2 cups mashed sweet potatoes (about 2 medium-sized sweet potatoes)
- 1/2 cup brown sugar
- 1/4 cup granulated sugar
- 1/4 cup melted butter
- 2 large eggs
- 1/2 cup evaporated milk
- 1 tsp vanilla extract
- 1 tsp ground cinnamon
- 1/2 tsp ground nutmeg
- 1/4 tsp ground ginger
- 1/4 tsp salt
- 1 unbaked pie crust

Directions

1. Make sure all ingredients are measured.

2. Turn oven to 350°F (175°C).

3. Wash the sweet potatoes and prick them several times with a fork. Place them on a baking sheet and bake for about 45-60 minutes or until they are tender. Allow them to cool slightly, then peel off the skins and mash the flesh until smooth. Set aside to cool completely.

4. In a large mixing bowl, combine the mashed sweet potatoes, brown sugar, granulated sugar, melted butter, eggs, evaporated milk, and vanilla extract. Mix until well combined.

5. Add the ground cinnamon, nutmeg, ginger, and salt to the sweet potato mixture, stirring until evenly incorporated.

6. Pour the filling into the unbaked pie crust, spreading it out evenly.

7. Bake the pie in the preheated oven for 50-60 minutes, or until the center is set and a knife inserted into the center comes out clean.

8. Remove the pie from the oven and allow it to cool completely before serving.

Apple Pie

Ingredients

- 6 cups thinly sliced apples (about 6 medium-sized apples, such as Granny Smith or Honeycrisp)
- 3/4 cup granulated sugar
- 2 Tbsp all-purpose flour
- 1 tsp ground cinnamon
- 1/4 tsp ground nutmeg
- 1/4 tsp salt
- 1 Tbsp lemon juice
- 2 Tbsp unsalted butter, cut into small pieces

For the pie crust:

Paired well with 1 pre-made or homemade pie crust, Chapter 4

Directions

1. Make sure all ingredients are measured.
2. Turn oven to 425°F (220°C).

3. In a large mixing bowl, combine the thinly sliced apples, granulated sugar, flour, cinnamon, nutmeg, salt, and lemon juice. Toss until the apples are evenly coated with the sugar and spices.

4. Roll out half of the pie crust and place it in the bottom of a 9-inch pie dish. Trim any excess dough, leaving about a 1-inch overhang.

5. Pour the apple filling into the prepared pie crust, spreading it out evenly. Dot the top of the filling with the small pieces of unsalted butter.

6. Roll out the remaining pie crust and place it over the top of the apple filling. Trim any excess dough, leaving about a 1-inch overhang. Fold the overhanging dough under the bottom crust and crimp the edges to seal.

7. Use a sharp knife to make several small slits or vents in the top crust to allow steam to escape during baking.

8. Optionally, you can brush the top crust with a little milk or beaten egg and sprinkle it with a bit of sugar for a golden finish.

9. Place the pie on a baking sheet (to catch any drips) and bake in the preheated oven for 45-50 minutes, or until the crust is golden brown and the filling is bubbly.

10. Remove the pie from the oven and allow it to cool on a wire rack for at least 1 hour before slicing and serving.

11. Serve slices of apple pie warm or at room temperature, with a scoop of vanilla ice cream or a dollop of whipped cream, if desired.

Apple Crumb Pie

Ingredients

For the pie filling:

- 6 cups thinly sliced apples (about 6 medium-sized apples, such as Granny Smith or Honeycrisp)
- 1/2 cup granulated sugar
- 1 Tbsp all-purpose flour
- 1 tsp ground cinnamon
- 1/4 tsp ground nutmeg
- 1/4 tsp salt
- 1 Tbsp lemon juice

For the crumb topping:

- 3/4 cup all-purpose flour
- 1/2 cup packed brown sugar
- 1/2 tsp ground cinnamon
- 1/4 cup unsalted butter, melted

For the pie crust:

Paired well with 1 pre-made or homemade pie crust, Chapter 4

Directions

1. Make sure all ingredients are measured.

2. Turn oven to 375°F (190°C).

3. In a large mixing bowl, combine the thinly sliced apples, granulated sugar, flour, cinnamon, nutmeg, salt, and lemon juice. Toss until the apples are evenly coated with the sugar and spices.

4. Roll out the pie crust and place it in the bottom of a 9-inch pie dish. Trim any excess dough, leaving about a 1-inch overhang.

5. Pour the apple filling into the prepared pie crust, spreading it out evenly.

For the crumb topping:

1. In a separate mixing bowl, combine the flour, brown sugar, and cinnamon. Stir until well mixed.

2. Pour the melted butter over the flour mixture and stir until the mixture resembles coarse crumbs.

3. Sprinkle the crumb topping evenly over the apple filling in the pie crust.

4. Place the pie on a baking sheet (to catch any drips) and bake in the preheated oven for 45-50 minutes, or until the crust is golden brown and the filling is bubbly.

5. Remove the pie from the oven and allow it to cool on a wire rack for at least 1 hour before slicing and serving.

6. Serve slices of apple crumb pie warm or at room temperature, with a scoop of vanilla ice cream or a dollop of whipped cream, if desired.

Pumpkin Pie

Ingredients

Pie filling:

- 1 (15-ounce) can of pumpkin puree (not pumpkin pie filling)
- 3/4 cup packed brown sugar
- 2 large eggs
- 1 cup evaporated milk
- 1 teaspoon vanilla extract
- 1 teaspoon ground cinnamon
- 1/2 teaspoon ground ginger
- 1/4 teaspoon ground nutmeg
- 1/4 teaspoon ground cloves
- 1/4 teaspoon salt

For the pie crust:

Paired well with 1 pre-made or homemade pie crust, Chapter 4

Directions

1. Make sure all ingredients are measured.

2. To make the pie crust, in a large mixing bowl, combine the flour, salt, and granulated sugar. Add the cold cubed butter and use a pastry cutter or your fingers to cut the butter into the flour mixture until it resembles coarse crumbs.

3. Gradually add the ice water, one tablespoon at a time, mixing with a fork until the dough comes together. Be careful not to overwork the dough. Shape the dough into a disc, wrap it in plastic wrap, and refrigerate for at least 30 minutes.

4. Turn oven to 375°F (190°C).

5. On a lightly floured surface, roll out the chilled pie dough into a circle about 12 inches in diameter. Carefully transfer the dough to a 9-inch pie dish, pressing it gently into the bottom and up the sides. Trim any excess dough and crimp the edges decoratively. Place the pie crust in the refrigerator while you prepare the filling.

6. In a large mixing bowl, whisk together the pumpkin puree, brown sugar, eggs, evaporated milk, vanilla extract, cinnamon, ginger, nutmeg, cloves, and salt until smooth and well combined.

7. Pour the pumpkin pie filling into the chilled pie crust, spreading it out evenly.

8. Place the pie on a baking sheet (to catch any drips) and bake in the preheated oven for 45-50 minutes, or until the filling is set and the crust is golden brown.

9. Remove the pie from the oven and allow it to cool completely on a wire rack before serving.

"Making Pie Motivation Time"

"Crafting a pie is about getting it right the first time. Everyone loves a delicious apple and sweet potato pie, but making something from scratch with your own hands allows you to embrace the journey of mishaps and personal growth. Allow yourself time to feel the wet dough go through your hands. Allow your apron to be fed with flour. Each new task allows you to gain a new experience. Be encouraged; creating a masterpiece takes time. The more you do something, the better you get.

You may get frustrated, and you might forget to double all the ingredients when trying to make a bigger batch, but please know every setback provides an opportunity to develop and a stepping stone towards victory.

So, if you're worried about messing up, I will burst your bubble by saying you will. We all have messed up a time or two. Doubting your ability is common; I still do. Give yourself grace, have patience with yourself, and sprinkle some determination when making your pie.

With that being said, roll up your sleeves, roll out your dough, fill your pies with your favorite fillings, and bake with all your heart. You've got this!"

– Shatia Godfrey

Peach Pie

Ingredients

Pie filling:

- 6 cups sliced fresh peaches (about 6-8 medium-sized peaches)
- 1/2 cup granulated sugar
- 1/4 cup packed brown sugar
- 3 Tbsp cornstarch
- 1 tsp ground cinnamon
- 1/4 tsp ground nutmeg
- 1/4 tsp salt
- 1 Tbsp lemon juice
- 1 tsp vanilla extract

For the topping:

- 1/2 cup all-purpose flour
- 1/2 cup packed brown sugar
- 1/4 cup rolled oats

- 1/4 tsp ground cinnamon
- 1/4 cup unsalted butter, cold and cut into small cubes

For the pie crust:

Paired well with 1 pre-made or homemade pie crust, Chapter 4

Directions

1. Make sure all ingredients are measured.

2. To make the pie crust, in a large mixing bowl, combine the flour, salt, and granulated sugar. Add the cold cubed butter and use a pastry cutter or your fingers to cut the butter into the flour mixture until it resembles coarse crumbs.

3. Gradually add the ice water, one tablespoon at a time, mixing with a fork until the dough comes together. Be careful not to overwork the dough. Shape the dough into a disc, wrap it in plastic wrap, and refrigerate for at least 30 minutes.

4. Turn oven to 375°F (190°C).

5. On a lightly floured surface, roll out the chilled pie dough into a circle about 12 inches in diameter. Carefully transfer the dough to a 9-inch pie dish, pressing it gently into the bottom and up the sides. Trim any excess dough and crimp the edges decoratively. Place the pie crust in the refrigerator while you prepare the filling.

6. In a large mixing bowl, combine the sliced peaches, granulated sugar, brown sugar, cornstarch, cinnamon, nutmeg, salt, lemon juice, and vanilla extract. Toss until the peaches are evenly coated.

7. Pour the peach filling into the prepared pie crust, spreading it out evenly.

8. In a separate mixing bowl, combine the flour, brown sugar, rolled oats, and ground cinnamon for the topping. Add the cold cubed butter and use a pastry cutter or your fingers to cut the butter into the flour mixture until it resembles coarse crumbs.

9. Sprinkle the topping evenly over the peach filling in the pie crust.

10. Place the pie on a baking sheet (to catch any drips) and bake in the preheated oven for 50-60 minutes, or until the crust is golden brown and the filling is bubbly.

11. Remove the pie from the oven and allow it to cool completely on a wire rack before serving.

12. Serve slices of peach pie warm or at room temperature, with a scoop of vanilla ice cream or a dollop of whipped cream, if desired.

Pecan Pie

Ingredients

Pie filling:

- 1 cup granulated sugar
- 3/4 cup dark corn syrup
- 3 large eggs
- 1 tsp vanilla extract
- 2 Tbsp unsalted butter, melted
- 1 1/2 cups pecan halves

For the pie crust:

Paired well with 1 pre-made or homemade pie crust, Chapter 4

Directions

1. Make sure all ingredients are measured.

2. To make the pie crust, in a large mixing bowl, combine the flour, salt, and granulated sugar. Add the cold cubed butter and use a pastry cutter or your fingers to cut the butter into the flour mixture until it resembles coarse crumbs.

3. Gradually add the ice water, one tablespoon at a time, mixing with a fork until the dough comes together. Be careful not to overwork the dough. Shape the dough into a disc, wrap it in plastic wrap, and refrigerate for at least 30 minutes.

4. Turn oven to 350°F (175°C).

5. On a lightly floured surface, roll out the chilled pie dough into a circle about 12 inches in diameter. Carefully transfer the dough to a 9-inch pie dish, pressing it gently into the bottom and up the sides. Trim any excess dough and crimp the edges decoratively. Place the pie crust in the refrigerator while you prepare the filling.

6. In a large mixing bowl, whisk together the granulated sugar, dark corn syrup, eggs, vanilla extract, and melted butter until well combined.

7. Arrange the pecan halves in the bottom of the chilled pie crust in an even layer.

8. Pour the pecan pie filling over the pecans, making sure they are evenly coated.

9. Place the pie on a baking sheet (to catch any drips) and bake in the preheated oven for 50-60 minutes, or until the filling is set and the crust is golden brown.

10. Remove the pie from the oven and allow it to cool completely on a wire rack before serving.

11. Serve slices of pecan pie with a dollop of whipped cream or a scoop of vanilla ice cream, if desired.

Lemon Meringue Pie

Ingredients

For the lemon filling:

- 1 cup granulated sugar
- 1/4 cup cornstarch
- 1/4 tsp salt
- 1 1/2 cups water
- 1/2 cup fresh lemon juice
- 3 large egg yolks
- 2 Tbsp unsalted butter
- Zest of 2 lemons

For the meringue:

- 3 large egg whites
- 1/4 tsp cream of tartar
- 1/2 cup granulated sugar

For the crust:

- 1 1/2 cups graham cracker crumbs
- 1/4 cup granulated sugar
- 1/3 cup melted butter

Directions

1. Make sure all ingredients are measured.

2. Turn oven to 350°F (175°C).

3. In a bowl, mix the graham cracker crumbs, sugar, and melted butter until well combined. Press the mixture firmly into the bottom and up the sides of a 9-inch pie dish. Bake the crust for 10 minutes, then remove it from the oven and let it cool.

4. For the lemon filling, in a saucepan, whisk together the sugar, cornstarch, and salt. Gradually whisk in the water and lemon juice until smooth. Cook over medium heat, stirring constantly, until the mixture thickens and boils. Boil for 1 minute, then remove from heat.

5. In a separate bowl, lightly beat the egg yolks. Gradually whisk in about 1/2 cup of the hot lemon mixture to temper the eggs, then pour the egg mixture back into the saucepan with the remaining lemon mixture. Cook and stir over low heat for 2 minutes.

6. Remove the lemon filling from the heat and stir in the butter and lemon zest until the butter is melted and the mixture is smooth. Pour the filling into the cooled crust.

7. For the meringue, in a clean bowl, beat the egg whites and cream of tartar with an electric mixer on high speed until soft peaks form. Gradually add the sugar, a tablespoon at a time, beating on high speed until stiff peaks form and the sugar is dissolved.

8. Spread the meringue over the hot lemon filling, making sure to seal the edges to prevent shrinking or weeping.

9. Bake the pie for 12 to 15 minutes or until the meringue is lightly browned. Cool the pie on a wire rack for 1 hour, then refrigerate for at least 3 hours before serving.

CHAPTER 7: GARNISHES

Picture your favorite dessert at your favorite restaurant or dessert parlor. Each plate is garnished with fresh fruit, edible flowers, or a sweet and delicate sauce. Each garnish adds a unique touch that compliments that craved confectioner. Sprinkles add a festive touch to any cake or cupcake, while 24-carat edible leaf adds a delicate yet luxurious element to any treat.

Garnishes add another dimension that entices the eye and the palate and unravels a journey of taste and textures, allowing each bite to be a humble treat. Garnishes had a sense of elevation that I can't wait to indulge in. The crunchy, creamy, and saucy texture unpacks joy to any sweet creation.

Strawberry Shortcake Crumble

Ingredients

For the Vanilla Crumble

- 1/2 stick of butter, softened (salted or unsalted)
- 1/2 cup of all-purpose flour
- 1 package (3 oz) of instant vanilla pudding mix

For the Strawberry crumble

- 1/2 stick of butter, softened
- 1/2 cup of all-purpose flour
- 1 package (3 oz) of strawberry Jell-O

Directions

1. Make sure all ingredients are measured.
2. Turn oven to 350 degrees Fahrenheit (175 degrees Celsius). Line a baking sheet pan with parchment paper.
3. In a bowl, combine the softened butter, flour, and instant vanilla pudding mix. Use your hands or a spoon to mix until crumbly.

4. In another bowl, mix the softened butter, flour, and strawberry Jell-O until crumbly.

5. Spread both mixtures evenly onto the parchment-lined baking dish.

6. Bake in the preheated oven for 8 minutes, then remove and allow to cool for 20 minutes. I prefer putting the crumble mix in the refrigerator.

7. Once cooled, break the baked mixture into crumbly chunks. I prefer using a food processor to crumble the mix.

8. Serve as a crunchy topping for desserts like strawberry shortcake, ice cream, or yogurt, or enjoy it on its own as a delicious snack.

Chocolate Eclair Crumble

Ingredients

For the Vanilla Crumble

- 1/2 stick of butter, softened (salted or unsalted)
- 1/2 cup of all-purpose flour
- 1 package (3 oz) of instant vanilla pudding mix

For the Chocolate Crumble

- 1/2 stick of butter, softened (salted or unsalted)
- 1/2 cup of all-purpose flour
- 1 package (3 oz) of instant chocolate pudding mix

Directions

1. Make sure all ingredients are measured.
2. Turn oven to 350 degrees Fahrenheit (175 degrees Celsius). Line a baking sheet pan with parchment paper.
3. In a bowl, combine the softened butter, flour, and instant vanilla pudding mix. Use your hands or a spoon to mix until crumbly.

127

4. In another bowl, mix the softened butter, flour, and chocolate pudding until crumbly.

5. Spread both mixtures evenly onto the parchment-lined baking dish.

6. Bake in the preheated oven for 8 minutes, then remove and allow to cool for 20 minutes. I prefer putting the crumble mix in the refrigerator.

7. Once cooled, break the baked mixture into crumbly chunks. I prefer using a food processor to crumble the mix.

8. Serve as a crunchy topping for desserts like chocolate éclair crumble, ice cream, or yogurt, or enjoy it on its own as a delicious snack.

Sweet Almond Crumble

Ingredients

- 1/2 stick of butter, softened (salted or unsalted)
- 1/2 cup of all-purpose flour
- 1 package (3 oz) of instant vanilla pudding mix
- 1/2 cup of almonds slivers

Directions

1. Make sure all ingredients are measured.

2. Turn oven to 350 degrees Fahrenheit (175 degrees Celsius). Line a baking sheet pan with parchment paper.

3. Place almonds in a food processor or use a knife and chop them into small pieces.

4. In a bowl, combine the softened butter, flour, instant vanilla pudding mix, and finely chopped almonds. Use your hands or a spoon to mix until crumbly.

5. Spread both mixtures evenly onto the parchment-lined baking dish.

6. Bake for 8 minutes, then remove and allow to cool for 20 minutes. I prefer putting the crumble mix in the refrigerator.

7. Once cooled, break the baked mixture into crumbly chunks. I prefer using a food processor to crumble the mix.

8. Serve as a crunchy topping for desserts like sweet almond crumble, ice cream, or yogurt, or enjoy it on its own as a delicious snack.

Toasted Almonds

Ingredients

- 1 cup of almonds

Directions

1. Make sure all ingredients are measured.

2. Turn oven to 350 degrees Fahrenheit (175 degrees Celsius). Line a baking sheet with parchment paper.

3. Place almonds on a baking sheet pan and bake for 7 to 8 minutes. The almonds should be golden brown.

4. Let cool and garnish your cake.

Toasted Coconut

Ingredients

- 1 bag of shredded coconut

Directions

1. Make sure all ingredients are measured.

2. Turn oven to 350 degrees Fahrenheit (175 degrees Celsius). Line a baking sheet with parchment paper.

3. Place shredded on a baking sheet pan and bake for 6 to 7 minutes, stirring the coconut every minute. Shredded coconut should be golden brown.

4. Let cool and garnish your cake.

CHAPTER 8: CAKE DECORATING TIPS

(Judith Conigliaro- High School baking teacher, Left, Tia, Right)

Welcome to my FAVORITE PART OF THE BAKING PROCESS: cake decorating. Cake decorating is where your creativity and imagination can be free. Please understand that cake decorating is not for the faint of heart. Mastery cannot be achieved in an instant. In fact, perfecting cake decorating techniques requires countless hours of practice and a high level of patience.

I remember vividly the times in high school when Mrs. Conigliaro would instruct us who were tasked for the day to each get a sheet pan. On that sheet pan we would practice making shell boarders, roses, rosettes, writing, and many different piping techniques. She would patiently guide us when we struggled with a technique. Back then and to this day, I still struggle with writing. I have awful handwriting, and my piping on a cake is no better. Thanks to many inventions like embossers, fondant, and Cricut, I am allowed to provide messages on a cake that's clean and consistent.

We would also practice icing cakes. I was so proud and honored that my decorating skills were stellar enough that Mrs. Conigliaro asked if I could create red roses for a 4-tiered square cake for the 232nd birthday of the U.S. Marines. Although all the bake shop classes had a part in creating the masterpiece. I was elated to have my roses as the centerpiece of my first decorated cake.

"Making Cake Decorating Motivation Time"

"Cake decorating is all about practice, practice, practice, and more practice. As you get the hang of things, you begin to understand how to position the piping bag and how much pressure you should use to release the buttercream.

When icing a cake, maybe it may not always be as smooth as you would like Honestly, my cakes may sometimes have air bubbles or slightly uneven. We're imperfect humans, and if you take a close look at yourself, there may be some imperfections with you.

So, embrace the inconsistencies in your piping and bumps when it comes to icing a cake. Remember, that this is new to you, and these are your humble beginnings that will flourish into stellar works of art.

Believe in this case that practice will make it alright. We're not shooting for perfect, not yet at least. We're doing this because we want to learn something new and we actually love this. It's about the dedication, belief, and passion that got us here in the first place. Someone inspired us. Just know that an amazing cake decorator who you admire once started at the stage at which you are now. We just see the final results of their practice. So, put your icing in your piping bag and be as creative as you want to be. Heck, mix colors together. And remember, You've got this!"

-Shatia Godfrey

How to Frost a Cake

Tools:

Buttercream frosting (in desired color)

Icing Spatula or Offset Spatula

Uniced Cake or Cake Dummy

1. Make sure your cake is completely cooled before you begin icing. Level the top of the cake if necessary to create a flat surface for icing.

2. Choose Your Frosting: Select your desired frosting for icing the cake. Buttercream, cream cheese frosting, and ganache are popular choices. Ensure your frosting is at a spreadable consistency.

3. Crumb Coat: Apply a thin layer of frosting all over the cake to seal in any crumbs. This layer acts as a base and helps the final layer of frosting to adhere smoothly. Use an offset spatula to spread the frosting evenly.

4. Chill the Cake: Place the cake in the refrigerator for about 15-30 minutes to allow the crumb coat to set. This will make it easier to apply the final layer of frosting without picking up crumbs.

5. Apply the Final Coat: Once the crumb coat has set, remove the cake from the refrigerator. Add a generous amount of frosting to the top

of the cake, then use an offset spatula to spread it evenly over the top and sides of the cake.

6. Smooth the Frosting: Use a bench scraper or offset spatula to smooth the frosting on the sides of the cake, starting from the top and working your way down. Hold the scraper or spatula at a slight angle to create a smooth finish.

7. Finish the Top: Once the sides of the cake are smooth, use the offset spatula to create a smooth finish on the top of the cake. Alternatively, you can create swirls or other decorative patterns with the spatula or piping bag.

8. Chill the Cake (Optional): If your frosting is prone to softening, you may want to chill the cake in the refrigerator for a short time to help the frosting set before serving.

How to Write on a Cake

Tools:

Buttercream frosting (in desired color)

Piping bag

Writing tip (Wilton #4 or similar)

Cake (already frosted and smoothed or a sheet pan for practice)

1. Prepare Your Piping Bag: Fit a piping bag with a small, round piping tip. Fill the piping bag with your desired frosting, making sure it's at room temperature for smooth piping.

2. Practice Your Lettering: Before piping onto your cake or cookies, practice writing the letters of the alphabet on a piece of parchment paper or a clean surface. This will help you get a feel for the pressure and flow of the frosting.

3. Plan Your Message: Decide what message you want to write on your cake or cookies and visualize how you want it to appear. You can lightly sketch the letters onto the surface with a toothpick as a guide if you're unsure.

4. Begin Piping: Start piping your message by holding the piping bag at a 45-degree angle to the surface. Gently squeeze the piping bag to release a steady stream of frosting as you trace over your sketched letters.

5. Maintain Consistent Pressure: Keep a steady hand and maintain consistent pressure on the piping bag as you pipe each letter. This will ensure uniformity in size and thickness throughout your message.

6. Space Letters Appropriately: Leave enough space between each letter to ensure clarity and readability. You can adjust the spacing as needed to fit your message onto the surface.

7. Connect Letters: When piping cursive or connected letters, be mindful of connecting strokes to maintain fluidity and legibility. Lift the piping bag slightly between letters to avoid dragging frosting across the surface.

8. Correct Mistakes: If you make a mistake while piping, don't panic! Simply use a toothpick or small spatula to gently remove any excess frosting and reshape the letter as needed.

9. Practice Patience: Take your time and focus on each letter individually, ensuring precision and accuracy in your piping. It's okay to work slowly and carefully to achieve the desired result.

How to Make Rosettes

Tools:

Buttercream frosting (in desired color)

Piping bag

Rose tip (Wilton #1M or similar)

Cake (already frosted and smoothed or a sheet pan for practice)

1. Prepare Your Piping Bag: Fit a piping bag with a large star-shaped piping tip. Fill the piping bag with your desired frosting, ensuring it's at room temperature for easy piping.

2. Practice Pressure: Hold the piping bag at a 90-degree angle to the surface of your cake or a practice surface. Practice applying even pressure to the piping bag to control the flow of frosting.

3. Create a Base: Start by piping a small dot of frosting onto the surface where you want the center of your rosette to be. This will act as the base for your rosette.

4. Pipe the Center: Position the piping tip slightly above the center dot of frosting. Apply gentle pressure to the piping bag and pipe a small, tight swirl of frosting around the center dot. This will form the center of your rosette.

5. Form the Petals: Continue piping swirls of frosting around the center, gradually moving outward in a circular motion. As you pipe each swirl, slightly overlap it with the previous one to create layered petals.

6. Control Size and Shape: Adjust the pressure on the piping bag to control the size and shape of the rosette. Apply more pressure for larger petals and less pressure for smaller petals.

7. Complete the Rosette: Continue piping petals until you've reached the desired size for your rosette. Once finished, release pressure on the piping bag and pull it away from the surface to create a clean finish.

8. Practice Makes Perfect: If you're new to piping rosettes, don't worry if they don't turn out perfectly the first time. Practice on a separate surface until you feel comfortable with the technique.

How to Make Roses

Tools:

Buttercream frosting (in desired color)

Piping bag

Rose tip (Wilton # 102, 103, 104 or similar)

Cake (already frosted and smoothed or a sheet pan for practice)

1. Gather Your Materials: You'll need icing in your desired colors, piping bags, a flower nail, parchment paper squares, and a petal tip (such as a Wilton #104).

2. Prepare the Icing: If you're making your own icing, ensure it's at the right consistency for piping. It should be thick enough to hold its shape but not too stiff. If it's too thick, add a few drops of water. If it's too thin, add powdered sugar.

3. Attach Parchment Paper to Flower Nail: Place a small dot of icing on the flower nail and stick a parchment paper square on top. This will allow you to easily transfer the roses to your cake later.

4. Fill Piping Bag: Fit your piping bag with the petal tip and fill it with your chosen icing color. Twist the top of the bag to secure the icing.

5. Create the Center Bud: Hold the piping bag at a 45-degree angle to the parchment paper. Squeeze out a small amount of icing while rotating the nail slightly. This forms the center bud of the rose.

6. Pipe the First Petal: Position the petal tip at the base of the center bud, with the wide end of the tip facing down and the narrow end facing up. Apply pressure to the piping bag while moving it in an upward motion to create the first petal.

7. Add More Petals: Continue piping petals around the center bud, overlapping each petal slightly with the previous one. Gradually angle the piping bag outward as you pipe to create a natural rose shape.

8. Build Layers: As you pipe more petals, vary the angle and pressure to create depth and dimension. Start with smaller petals near the center and gradually increase the size as you work outward.

9. Finish the Rose: Once you've reached your desired size, stop piping and gently pull the piping bag away to release the icing. You can use a small spatula or toothpick to smooth out any rough edges.

10. Let the Roses Set: Allow the icing roses to set at room temperature for at least 4-6 hours or until they are firm enough to handle.

11. Transfer to Cake: Carefully peel the parchment paper squares from the back of the roses and place them on your cake using a small amount of fresh icing as "glue."

How to Make a Shell Border

Tools:

Buttercream frosting (in desired color)

Piping bag

Shell tip (Wilton #16, 32, 4B, 1M, or similar)

Cake (already frosted and smoothed or a sheet pan for practice)

1. Prepare Your Piping Bag: Fit your piping bag with the shell piping tip. Make sure the tip is secure at the end of the bag, and trim any excess bag if necessary.

2. Fill the Piping Bag: Spoon your desired buttercream frosting into the piping bag. Fill it about halfway full to ensure easy handling and less mess.

3. Hold the Piping Bag Properly: Hold the piping bag at a 45-degree angle to the cake, with the wide end of the tip touching the surface of the cake.

4. Start Piping: Squeeze the piping bag gently to release frosting while moving your hand in a zigzag motion. Begin piping a shell shape by applying even pressure to the bag, then releasing the pressure as you pull the bag away to form a tapered end.

5. Continue Piping: Pipe another shell shape right next to the first one, slightly overlapping the tails of the shells to create a continuous border.

6. Maintain Consistency: Try to maintain a consistent size and shape for each shell. Practice on a separate surface if needed to get a feel for the pressure and movement required.

7. Complete the Border: Continue piping shells around the entire perimeter of the cake until you reach the starting point. Make sure to space them evenly for a uniform look.

8. End Smoothly: To finish the border, stop piping just before reaching the starting point. Taper off the frosting by gradually reducing pressure on the piping bag and lifting it away from the cake.

9. Smooth Out Any Imperfections: Use a small offset spatula or a clean finger to gently smooth out any rough edges or imperfections in the shells.

10. Final Touches: If desired, you can add small decorative touches such as sugar pearls or sprinkles to enhance the border.

11. Chill if Necessary: If the cake needs to be refrigerated before serving, place it in the refrigerator to allow the frosting to set before serving.

12. Enjoy Your Beautiful Cake: Once the frosting has set, your cake with a shell border is ready to be served and enjoyed!

APPENDIX

Dry Ingredients:
1 cup = 240 mL
1/2 cup = 120 mL
1/3 cup = 80 mL
1/4 cup = 60 mL
1/8 cup = 30 mL
1 tablespoon = 15 mL
1 teaspoon = 5 mL
1/2 teaspoon = 2.5 mL
1/4 teaspoon = 1.25 mL

Liquid Ingredients:
1 cup = 240 mL
1/2 cup = 120 mL
1/3 cup = 80 mL
1/4 cup = 60 mL
1/8 cup = 30 mL
1 tablespoon = 15 mL

1 teaspoon = 5 mL	

1/2 teaspoon = 2.5 mL

1/4 teaspoon = 1.25 mL

Butter/Margarine:

1 stick = 1/2 cup = 113 grams

1/2 stick = 1/4 cup = 56.5 grams

1/4 stick = 2 tablespoons = 28.5 grams

1 tablespoon = 14.2 grams

Sugar:

1 cup granulated sugar = 200 grams

1 cup packed brown sugar = 220 grams

1 cup powdered sugar = 120 grams

1 tablespoon honey = 21 grams

1 tablespoon maple syrup = 20 grams

Flour:

1 cup all-purpose flour = 120 grams

1 cup cake flour = 115 grams

1 cup whole wheat flour = 130 grams

1 cup bread flour = 130 grams	

Baking Powder:
1 teaspoon = 4 grams

Baking Soda:
1 teaspoon = 5 grams

"Pints pounds the world is round, pints and pounds are equal."

– Judith Conigliaro

TYPES OF FLOUR AND USES

1. **All-Purpose Flour:**

   - Use: A go-to flour for many baked goods, such as cakes, cookies, and breads. When using this flour for cakes, the cake crumb is likely to be coarse.

   - Properties: Contains a moderate protein level (10-12%), providing a balance of strength and tenderness.

2. **Bread Flour:**

   - Use: Ideal for yeast breads and pizza dough.

   - Properties: High protein content (12-14%), which helps create a chewy texture and good rise.

3. **Cake Flour:**

   - Use: Perfect for making cakes, muffins, and other delicate baked items. When using this flour for cakes, the cake crumb tends to be velvety.

   - Properties: Low protein level (6-8%), resulting in a very fine, soft crumb.

4. **Pastry Flour:**

   - Use: Best suited for pie crusts, biscuits, and pastries.

   - Properties: Medium protein content (8-9%), providing a balance of flakiness and tenderness.

5. **Whole Wheat Flour:**

   - Use: Adds a rich, nutty flavor to whole-grain breads and baked goods.

   - Properties: Contains bran and germ, offering higher fiber and nutrients and giving a denser texture.

6. **Self-Rising Flour:**

   - Use: Convenient for quick breads, biscuits, and pancakes.

   - Properties: Pre-mixed with baking powder and salt, eliminating the need for additional leavening agents.

7. **Rye Flour:**

   - Use: Traditional ingredient in rye bread and sourdough.

   - Properties: Lower gluten content, resulting in a dense texture and unique flavor.

8. **Almond Flour:**

   - Use: Popular in gluten-free baking, adding moisture and a nutty taste.

   - Properties: Made from finely ground almonds, rich in fat and low in carbohydrates.

9. **Coconut Flour:**

   - Use: Used in gluten-free and low-carb recipes.

   - Properties: High in fiber and absorbs a lot of liquid, often requiring extra eggs or liquids.

10. **Oat Flour:**

    - Use: Adds a mild, sweet flavor to baked goods and is often used in gluten-free recipes.

    - Properties: Made from ground oats, high in fiber and slightly sweet.

11. **Semolina Flour:**

    - Use: Essential for pasta and some breads and desserts.

    - Properties: Coarse flour from durum wheat, providing a firm texture.

12. **Buckwheat Flour:**

    - Use: Ideal for pancakes, waffles, and certain breads.

    - Properties: Gluten-free with a strong, earthy taste.

13. **Spelt Flour:**

    - Use: Adds a nutty flavor to breads and pastries.

    - Properties: An ancient grain with a gluten structure like wheat but often easier to digest.

14. Rice Flour:

- Use: Common in gluten-free baking and for thickening sauces.

- Properties: Made from finely milled rice, producing a light texture and mild flavor.

15. Chickpea Flour (Garbanzo Bean Flour):

- Use: Used in gluten-free baking and as a thickener for soups and sauces.

- Properties: Made from ground chickpeas, high in protein and fiber, with a slightly nutty flavor.

GLOSSARY

All-purpose Flour: A versatile flour suitable for a variety of baking recipes. It has a moderate protein content, usually around 10-12%.

Baking Powder: A leavening agent made from a combination of an acid (like cream of tartar) and a base (such as baking soda). It releases carbon dioxide when moistened and heated, helping baked goods rise.

Baking Soda: A leavening agent also known as sodium bicarbonate. It requires an acidic ingredient in the recipe (such as buttermilk or lemon juice) to activate and produce carbon dioxide for leavening.

Blind Baking: The process of pre-baking a pie crust or pastry shell before filling it, often done with weights to prevent puffing.

Bloom: The process of softening gelatin in a liquid before it is melted and added to a recipe. This ensures even distribution and prevents clumping.

Cream of Tartar: A byproduct of winemaking used in baking to stabilize egg whites, prevent sugar crystallization, and act as a leavening agent when combined with baking soda.

Crumb: The texture and structure of the inside of baked goods, such as bread or cake. A good crumb is typically moist, tender, and evenly aerated.

Crumb Coat: A thin layer of icing applied to a cake to trap crumbs and create a smooth surface for the final layer of icing. It helps to keep crumbs out of the final decoration.

Dock: The act of pricking pastry dough with a fork before baking to prevent it from puffing up and to allow steam to escape.

Egg Wash: A mixture of beaten egg and liquid (usually water or milk) brushed on dough before baking to give it a shiny, golden-brown finish.

Ferment: Allowing dough to rest and rise, typically with yeast, to develop flavor and structure. This is an essential step in bread making.

Fermentation: The process by which yeast converts sugars into carbon dioxide and alcohol, causing dough to rise and develop flavor.

Folding: A gentle mixing technique used to combine light ingredients (like whipped cream or beaten egg whites) with heavier mixtures, preserving air and volume.

Fusion Method: Also known as the Blend-phase Technique. Combines different traditional techniques to maximize flavor and texture, integrating ingredients in stages.

Ganache: A rich mixture of chocolate and cream, used as a filling, icing, or glaze. It can be poured over cakes for a smooth, shiny finish or whipped to a lighter consistency.

Glaze: A glossy coating applied to baked goods, made from sugar and liquid (such as water, milk, or fruit juice). It can be thin and transparent or thicker and opaque, depending on the desired effect.

Gluten: A protein found in wheat flour that provides elasticity and strength to dough. It helps trap air bubbles during rising, contributing to the structure and chewiness of baked goods.

Hydration: The amount of water in a dough or batter relative to the flour. High hydration doughs are often wetter and stickier, yielding a more open crumb.

Icing: A sweet, often creamy glaze made of sugar with a liquid, such as water or milk, that is typically used to cover or decorate baked goods.

Kneading: The process of working dough to develop gluten. This can be done by hand or with a mixer and involves stretching and folding the dough repeatedly.

Laminate: To create layers in dough by folding butter into it, as seen in puff pastry and croissants. This process results in flaky, airy baked goods.

Leaven: To cause dough or batter to rise by incorporating air or gas, typically with yeast, baking powder, or baking soda. Leavening creates a lighter, more tender texture in baked goods.

Leavening Agent: Ingredients used to produce gas in dough or batter, causing it to rise. Common leavening agents include yeast, baking powder, and baking soda.

Macerate: To soak fruit in liquid (often sugar, alcohol, or a combination) to soften it and enhance its flavor.

Meringue: A mixture of whipped egg whites and sugar baked until crisp. Meringue can be used as a topping for pies, as a base for desserts, or shaped into cookies.

Piping: The technique of using a pastry bag fitted with a nozzle to shape or decorate dough, batter, or icing. Commonly used for cookies, cakes, and pastries.

Proof: The final rise of shaped dough before baking. This step allows the dough to develop its final volume and texture.

Retarding: Slowing down the fermentation process by refrigerating dough. This technique is used to enhance flavor and timing flexibility.

Ripple Method: Also known as the Wave-fold Technique. Ensures even distribution of ingredients while maintaining aeration, resulting in a light, tender cake texture.

Scalding: Heating a liquid (usually milk) to just below boiling and then cooling it, often to denature proteins and improve texture in baked goods.

Scoring: Making shallow cuts on the surface of bread dough before baking. This allows controlled expansion and creates decorative patterns.

Silk-blend Technique: Also known as the Velvet Method. Focuses on gradual ingredient incorporation and low-speed mixing to create a smooth, velvety batter.

Soft Peaks: The stage in beating egg whites or cream when the mixture forms peaks that softly bend over without holding their shape.

Sponge: A light, airy cake made by whipping eggs and sugar until thick and pale, then folding in flour and other ingredients. The high volume of whipped eggs creates its characteristic light texture.

Stabilize: To add an ingredient (such as cream of tartar or cornstarch) to a mixture to maintain its texture and prevent it from breaking down. Commonly done with whipped cream or egg whites.

Stiff Peaks: The stage in beating egg whites or cream when the mixture forms peaks that stand upright without collapsing.

Tempering: Gradually bringing ingredients to the same temperature before combining them, preventing curdling or seizing. This is often used with eggs or chocolate.

Turn: In laminated doughs, a turn refers to rolling out the dough and folding it in thirds or quarters to create layers. Multiple turns are done to create many thin layers.

Velvet Method: Also known as the Silk Blend Technique. Focuses on gradual ingredient incorporation and low-speed mixing to create a smooth, velvety batter.

Whip: To beat ingredients, such as cream or egg whites, at high speed to incorporate air and increase volume. Whipping creates a light, airy texture.

Windowpane Test: A method to check if bread dough has been kneaded enough by stretching a small piece into a thin membrane. If it stretches without tearing, gluten is well-developed.

ABOUT THE AUTHOR

Shatia Godfrey

My love for baking started in my grandmother's kitchen, where I spent countless hours watching her make delicious desserts from scratch. Her dedication and creativity ignited a lifelong passion for baking and inspired me to pursue it as a career. When I was young, I helped her sell her baked goods outside her apartment building, where I learned the value of hard work and the joy of sharing our creations with others.

I attended Mergenthaler Vocational Technical Senior High School, specializing in baking, and graduated in 2005. Eager to improve my skills, I enrolled at Baltimore International College, where I earned an Associate in Professional Baking and Applied Science. My first baking job was at Safeway Market, where I quickly formed a close bond with my coworker, Ms. Pam. Together, we baked and decorated cakes on the side, sharing techniques and recipes. Sadly, after Ms. Pam's passing, I took a ten-year break from baking and decorating.

In 2018, I decided to return to college and enrolled at Strayer University, earning my MBA in 2023. This education reignited my entrepreneurial spirit, and in 2019, I founded Tia Sweet Tooth LLC. Working from home, I specialize in creating custom cakes and cupcakes that bring joy to my clients.

My dream is to one day open a physical store where I can expand my business and continue making sweet memories for all my clients. Through hard work and dedication, I am committed to turning this dream into reality.

"Every cake I bake is a blend of love, passion, and the sweet memories from my grandmother's kitchen and all the amazing people who have added to this journey. Their legacy lives on in every creation."

– Shatia Godfrey

www.ingramcontent.com/pod-product-compliance
Lightning Source LLC
Chambersburg PA
CBHW080957120626
46546CB00010B/2939